# MANAGING
# Little
# League.
# BASEBALL

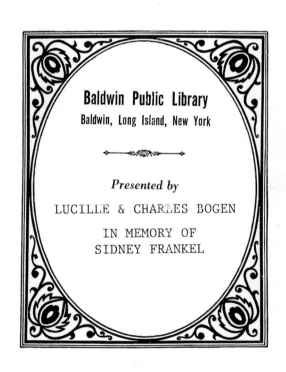

# MANAGING
# Little
# League®
# BASEBALL
## Ned McIntosh

Foreword by
**Chuck Tanner**
*Manager,* Atlanta Braves

CONTEMPORARY
**BOOKS, INC.**
CHICAGO

**Library of Congress Cataloging in Publication Data**

McIntosh, Ned.
    Managing little league baseball

    Includes index.
    1. Little League Baseball, inc.    2. Baseball for
children—United States—Coaching.    I. Title.
GV880.5.M34      1985        796.357′62        84-29385
ISBN 0-8092-5322-4

Photos by Nicholas Photography, Don Deitz, and Leo Rourke

Published by Contemporary Books, Inc.
180 North Michigan Avenue, Chicago, Illinois 60601
Manufactured in the United States of America
Library of Congress Catalog Card Number: 84-29385
International Standard Book Number: 0-8092-5322-4

Published simultaneously in Canada by Beaverbooks, Ltd.
195 Allstate Parkway, Valleywood Business Park
Markham, Ontario L3R 4T8 Canada

Dedicated to my sons, Bob, Tom, and Jim, who gave me the opportunity to be a Little League father/coach and the wonderful father-and-son relationships that inspired the writing of this book.

# CONTENTS

# FOREWORD

As the manager of the Atlanta Braves, having just arrived from the Pittsburgh Pirates, I hear many testimonials to Little League baseball from Major League ball players, to add to my own. But most books on coaching baseball are so complex that it seems like they are dedicated to teaching *all* children how to become Major League ball players, not acknowledging that a very small percentage will ever go that far in their careers. And, unfortunately, many would-be Little League coaches are discouraged by thinking that they must be baseball experts in order to coach a Little League team.

So it is refreshing to see this new book, dedicated to teaching the average boy or girl enough fundamentals of the game to really enjoy it and teaching the average Little League coach, who is usually the father of one of the players, how to make the game enjoyable to the youngsters he coaches and to himself.

The author, Ned McIntosh, has had a love affair with baseball and the Pittsburgh Pirates since he was a boy growing up in the East End of Pittsburgh. After he married and was blessed with a large family of three boys and three girls, he had the opportunity of furthering that love of baseball and sharing it with his children

Chuck Tanner and some of the Little League Giants take a break during practice.

and their teammates as a Little League coach. Out of that experience, he has developed a Little League coaching philosophy of "teach the basics and make it fun" that I heartily endorse.

If your child is blessed with exceptional athletic ability that may take him or her into higher levels of baseball—high school, college, or professional ball—he or she will have plenty of time at each successive level to work at learning the more intricate techniques of baseball. But at the Little League age level, it should be fun—not work—if you want a youngster's first exposure to our country's number one sport to be enjoyable. So teaching the fundamentals of baseball and combining it in a fun experience for his players are the best objectives a part-time coach should strive to achieve, and they are the objectives of this book.

The book also speaks to the potential problems of Little League baseball—such as competitive pressure and problem parents—and puts them in their proper perspective. But most of all, it lays out a sound, easy-to-follow plan of coaching that will make the father/coach enjoy Little League as much as his players and will give him the unique experience of doing something with his son or daughter—sharing the victories and defeats—that he will cherish all his life. If you are the parent of a boy or girl in Little League, and/or a Little League coach, I recommend this book to help you and your players get the most out of your Little League experience.

For the best in baseball for you and your children,

Chuck Tanner
Manager, Atlanta Braves

# INTRODUCTION

It was 2:00 A.M., and I couldn't sleep. That wasn't too unusual on a night when my Little League team had won an important game. The exhilaration of winning and the reliving of the exciting moments of the game always produced a high that made sleep difficult. But tonight was somehow different; there was something else working on me—something unsettling—that was keeping me awake.

Maybe it was the natural letdown after the final week of our Little League season, a week that saw everything go our way: the championship of our league; the honor of having four of our boys chosen for the All-Star team, including my son Jim; and then the county championship tonight, won in an exciting, extra-inning, error-free ball game—Little League baseball at its best!

But those were all reasons to be up, not down, so why the unsettling feeling? Suddenly I realized what it was. After 15 years of coaching three sons in Little League baseball, I had just coached my youngest son in his last Little League game.

Not only had that father/son, coach/player relationship spanned three sons and 15 years; it had also covered three different leagues in three different states, as my work moved me around the country. In that respect, my experience was somewhat unique, but I found that the situation of a father coaching his son's Little League team is much more common than unique in Little Leagues across the country. In our current 10-team league, 9 of the managers have sons on their respective teams, and the 10th has a daughter!

Frequently the only qualification required of a father to become a coach is having a son who wants to play baseball. "Your son won't be able to play," I remember being told when I took my middle son, Tom, to register, "unless we can find a dad to coach his team." Experience, playing or coaching, not required. I have met a few frustrated Billy Martins as Little League managers, but for the most part they were fathers, untrained and inexperienced in their coaching role, with only one thing in common: a son or daughter who wanted to play Little League baseball.

Not only does the new father/coach have to accept a quick-study assignment in managing a Little League team, but in addition he has to accept a relationship with his child that will become very rewarding and satisfying at its best and very frustrating and counterproductive at its worst.

In my initial experience as a father/coach, I devoured every piece of literature published by Little League headquarters and found them helpful. I also found many books on teaching the mechanics of playing *adult* baseball: i.e., hitting, pitching, fielding, etc. But I found little to prepare me for the challenges peculiar to Little League, such as participating in a player draft, keeping 15 boys busy and having fun at the same time in practice, moving players out of a lineup and back in again in conformance with mandatory playing rules, dealing with problem parents, helping boys cope with their first taste of competitive pressure, and all of the other problems that are uniquely part of Little League. Nor could I find a book written *by* a father/coach *for* other father/coaches.

I had no experience or training for the father/coach assignment, so my oldest son, Bob, now married and a young lawyer, and my middle son, Tom, just entering college, suffered from my inexperience and my mistakes. But by the time Jim, the youngest, had played his three years in Little League, I finally had my father/coach act together. Since most father/coaches don't have the opportunity to learn by trial and error with three sons, I wondered if my development of a philosophy, a practice routine, and a practical program for a dad to coach his child's team—spawned over 15 years and three sons—could help some other dads gain the best from their mutual Little League careers with their children.

So, at two o'clock in the morning, realizing that I would never again enjoy the pleasures, nor endure the frustrations, of coaching my son's Little League team, I found myself speculating as to whether I could help other father/coaches by sharing my experiences with them. Pretty heavy thinking for a nonwriter to contemplate at two in the morning, so I went back to bed, convinced that my urge to write a book, like my insomnia, would disappear by morning.

But it didn't. And now, three years later, the book that was conceived that night has finally been completed. In the ensuing years, my youngest son, Jim, has moved up to Senior League to prove to us both that he can make it on his own, and I have continued to manage a Little League team. It hasn't been quite the same, without a son on my team for the first time in 15 years, but it has given me an opportunity to reflect on what a truly unique father and son or daughter relationship coaching your child's team can be, sharing in the hard work, the wins and the losses, that you and your boy or girl will always remember.

If you have the rare privilege offered to you to coach your son or daughter's Little League team, seize it, relish it, enjoy it. Life is too short, and he or she will be young too briefly for you to miss this rare opportunity to do something together.

# 1
# CHOOSING YOUR PLAYERS

If you are new to Little League, a brief overview of the organization may be appropriate at this point. Little League Baseball, Incorporated, was started in 1939 and was granted a Congressional Charter of Federal Incorporation in 1964—the only sports organization that has ever been so honored by our government. If you become a Little League manager or coach, you will join an international group of managers and coaches that work with 49,000 Little League teams and 98,000 Minor League teams, serving 2.5 million children in 24 countries!

The local league is the governing body in any community and it is chartered each year by Little League Baseball, Incorporated, headquartered in Williamsport, Pennsylvania, where the World Series of Little League Baseball is held each August.

The president of a local league has the responsibility, with the guidance of a board of directors, to appoint the managers and coaches of all teams in his organization. If a league is fully structured within the Little League organization, it will include Little League baseball teams for youngsters ages 9 through 12; minor league "farm" teams for 8-year-olds and older players not selected for Little League teams; and T-Ball teams for beginning players as young as 6 years old. T-Ball teams overlap in age consideration with Minor League teams, which in turn overlap with Little League teams. In this way, players are able to compete at their own ability level, rather than strictly on the basis of age.

At the higher level, there is Senior League for players age 13 through 15 and Big League for players 16 through 18 years of age. Little League Softball was added in 1974. Little League Softball is played entirely by girls, and also includes Senior League and Big League teams, for the same ages as the baseball divisions.

The information in this book is designed to be helpful for coaches and managers of all Little League Baseball, Incorporated, divisions, regardless of the level of the team.

If you are a newly appointed manager, your first important decisions will involve selecting prospects for your team in the player draft. They will be decisions relating to your team's success and/or frustrations. The boy you could have had, but didn't pick, will come back to haunt you (for four years if he is a 9-year-old), and the boy you did pick, but shouldn't have, will create frustrations for you (also for four years if he is a 9-year-old).

Throughout the book the titles "manager" and "coach" are used interchangeably, since coaching is done by both. Officially, however, the manager is in charge of the team and responsible to the League President; and the coaches are the manager's assistants.

Throughout this book, I refer to "boys" and "sons" with no slight intended to "girls" and "daughters." I am merely acknowledging the fact that the success of the Little League Softball program is filtering nearly all of the girls out of Little League baseball. In the pre-Softball years, some of the best players in Little League baseball were girls, in part because of the physiological fact that girls mature faster than boys. So, if a girl signs up for baseball, as a few still do, don't overlook her as a draft pick. She could be good! Since I have three daughters as well as three sons, I can assure you that I am not biased toward boys in Little League. And if you are coaching your daughter's softball team, I think you may find this book helpful as well.

## THE DRAFT SYSTEM

I will assume that your league uses one of the draft systems recommended by Little League, preceded by formal registration and tryouts under the direction of the league player agent. As a manager, you will not be doing all you should do to prepare for the important player selection process if you merely wait for tryout day and assume you will see all that you need to see then to make your draft choices. Just as the professional baseball teams use scouts and do some research prior to their player draft, so should you.

## USING SCOUTS

Scouts? The returning members of your team are your best scouts, and I always have several meetings of them prior to the draft. I give them specific assignments by school, grade, and class to recommend new boys who may have moved into the area, as well as other boys who did not play for a Little League team last year. The latter group will include boys who played in the minors and boys who, for whatever reasons, have never played in organized ball but nevertheless appear to be good athletes. It is not uncommon for an 11- or 12-year-old boy to play Little League baseball for the first time. Perhaps he forgot to register the previous year, had no buddies who were playing, had transportation problems, didn't think he would like it, or, for any number of other reasons, didn't get involved. But when one of your scouts goes to work on him, and the boy realizes that he is wanted, he may decide this is the year he wants to play baseball.

If a boy is good, you will hear about it! Obviously, you won't get all of the good prospects, since they will be known to the other managers, too, but you owe it to your team to know who they are and to pick them if you have the chance. The sequence of the player selection is usually planned in favor of the weaker team; i.e., last place team picks first, and so on. Whenever it is your turn to pick, however, you may lose the opportunity to strengthen your team if you don't have a line on the best prospects.

Another obvious system of scouting (also used by the professionals) is watching the Minor League teams play. Time often prevents this, however, since they are playing on the same schedule as your Little League. The next best thing is to call the managers of the Minor League teams and ask for their advice about the best prospects for Little League. I ask for their recommendations of players not only from their respective teams, but from the opposing teams as well. I usually finish by asking them who, in their opinion, will be the top 10 boys picked from the Minors in the draft next year. I recommend that you make such calls at the end of the season, while their memories are still fresh.

Local school coaches are another source of helpful scouting information. They see the boys in physical education classes and intramural games and have an experienced, professional eye for spotting good potential athletes. And still another scouting opportunity is watching the other competitive sports teams in action. I watch the midget football games and basketball league games, keep an eye open for well-coordinated boys, and make a note of their names. Any new athletes who have moved into the area will usually show up in the lineup of a football team or basketball team in the fall and winter competitive leagues.

The final scouting source I use is the new boys at Little League registration. One year I saw a gangling 11-year-old boy signing up and asked him if he had played before. He said he had played for a Little League team in another town and had just moved here. I noticed that his baseball mitt was well worn, and I sensed he was a ball player, even though he was nothing but arms and legs in tryouts. Before he finished his Little League career, he turned into one of the best pitchers in the league and an All Star. The baseball mitt is a good clue, incidentally. If it is worn and dirty, the chances are its owner likes baseball and uses it a lot; if it is brand-new, be wary.

## TRYOUTS

Obviously, the tryouts will give you a final look at your prospects in action, and I treat it exactly that way: as a *final* look. Prior to the tryouts, you should have your prospect list made up and ranked in order of choice. The number of boys trying out, how well the tryouts are organized, and the weather will dictate how good your appraisal opportunity will be. I have seen tryouts that were a mass confusion of cold, jacket-clad boys going through the motions of throwing, catching, running, and batting, where little, if anything, could be determined of their relative abilities.

If brothers are trying out at the same time, or if you know that a good 10-year-old prospect has a good 8-year-old brother, keep the "brother rule" in mind; i.e., you have first option on a younger

Chuck Tanner talks baseball strategy with the author; his Little League captain, Chad O'Dell; and the author's son Jim, now a Senior League player.

brother in the current or a future draft. The younger brother of a good player who has graduated from Little League would normally be a good prospect, too, since he has the advantage of having an experienced brother to work out with him. (He will usually be one of your prospects with a dirty, well-used glove.)

If the son of a Minor League manager or coach is coming up in the draft, that could represent a double bonus for you. Not only do you get a boy with a dad who is dedicated and will work with him; you also have the opportunity of picking up another coach for your team. (Most Minor League coaches lose interest in the Minors when their sons make it to Little League).

## RULES OF THE DRAFT

If you are a new manager, it is important that you know the rules (local as well as national) regarding the player draft. They are not easily accessible, since they do not appear in the *Little League Baseball Official Regulations and Playing Rules.* The official regulations regarding player selection appear in the *Little League Baseball Handbook and Manual,* usually referred to as the "president's manual," since it is issued to league presidents. Your league president can review the official rules with you and should bring you up to date on any local rules. In particular, you should ask him to review with you:

1. The player selection method used by your league (the draft system, the auction system, or some local variation);
2. the provisions regarding drafting the sons of managers or coaches;
3. the provisions regarding drafting brothers;
4. the provisions regarding trading of players.

There are other considerations, not covered by the official rules, that you should inquire about before the player selection begins:

1. What about boys who did not register but apply after the draft? How are they drafted? They may have legitimate reasons for not registering, e.g., sickness, just moving to the area, etc.
2. What about boys who did register but don't show up for tryouts? There could be legitimate reasons for this as well.
3. What about boys who are drafted but never show up for your team practice?

I had a sticky situation involving a case like this, in which the boy I drafted had some buddies on another team and wanted to play only for that team. The president's manual appears to cover this situation when it states, "Each player acquired shall for the duration of their major Little League career be the property of the team making the acquisition, unless subsequently traded or released." I suggested a trade to the manager of the other team, but he wasn't interested, so unfortunately the boy didn't play. Although technically I did release him when I turned in my official roster, the board of directors of our league ruled that he would be considered a draft choice of mine the next year, without my having to forfeit another draft choice. To have ruled otherwise would violate the integrity of the draft system by allowing players to influence which team they should play for, directly or indirectly.

## DESIGNING A TEAM

In deciding your ranking of prospects in the draft, you naturally must keep in mind the strengths and weaknesses of your team, based on the returning players. If your team is a certain contender, you might want to choose a good 12-year-old who just moved in to strengthen your chance of winning the championship. On the other hand, if you are going into a rebuilding year, you might want to pass over the 12-year-old in favor of a good 10-year-old who will give you three years of increasingly good play.

Pitching considerations are, of course, very important since good pitching is key to the success of any winning team. (I have never seen a championship Little League team without at least two good pitchers.) Otherwise I use the "strong up the middle" rule, i.e., go for a potentially strong catcher, pitcher, shortstop, second baseman, and/or center fielder. A team that is strong up the middle will usually be a winner.

## TRADING PLAYERS

Although there are provisions for trading players in Little League, I recommend against it, particularly with established players. The feelings of the boys involved must be considered, and a boy who played for one team last year but is traded to another team this year could be treated like a turncoat by his former teammates, even though he had nothing to do with the trade. Children's criticism of each other can often be cruel.

Little League rules wisely restrict trades that do occur to a one-on-one basis (one player for one player) and require that they be consummated within the two-week period following the draft. Although there are undoubtedly legitimate extenuating reasons for a trade, a league would be wise to investigate thoroughly the reasons and the feelings of the boys involved to make certain that the integrity of its draft system is not being compromised. A manager who attempts to negotiate trades solely for the purpose of winning, and without regard to the feelings of the boys involved, is not adhering to the philosophy of "the boy comes first," which I think is implicit in Little League.

As soon as the draft is completed, you will naturally want to advise the boys of their selection by your team and schedule your first practice. In the next chapter, I point out that lack of good communications can create misunderstandings on the part of new boys and their parents regarding the draft and the final selection of players for the team. In that chapter, I also recommend that you prepare a letter for each new boy to take home to his parents after the first practice. It explains in a positive way the selection procedure, assures every boy that he will have an opportunity to play (if not for your Little League team this year, then for a Minor League team for his own development). At the same time, it establishes the goal of making the team as something so special that each boy will go all out to achieve it.

# 2
# STICK TO THE BASICS AND DRILL THEM

Baseball is a very complicated game, particularly in the comprehension of a 9- to 12-year-old. Recently a friend of mine from Australia came to visit, and I took him to see his first American-style baseball game. He was soon asking questions that made me realize how complicated our game of baseball is for a beginner, even an adult beginner, to understand. "How can he strike out when he didn't even swing at the ball?" he asked about a batter who had looked at a called third strike. "If a foul ball is a strike and three strikes are out, why isn't the batter out when he hits three foul balls?" he asked. "Because," I answered, "it doesn't count on the third strike, unless of course the foul on the third strike is caught by the catcher, in which case it is called a foul tip, and the batter is out." The look I got was like so many I have received from my Little League players when I have tried to explain a complicated rule or point of baseball strategy. It convinced me again that baseball is a very complicated game to a beginner.

Just explaining the rules and regulations of Little League baseball requires 64 pages of very small type in the *Little League Rule Book,* and there are enough books on the mechanics of

9

playing baseball to fill a library. The best instructional manual on baseball I have found is *The Complete Baseball Handbook,* by Walter Alston and Don Weiskopf (1972, Allyn and Bacon, Inc., Boston), $19.95, but it contains 567 pages of text and illustrations! A dad, whose primary qualification to coach is having a son who wants to play baseball, would be frightened off by the apparent complexity of the game if he didn't realize two important facts: (1) He is dealing with children who know less than he does. (2) The limited amount of time he has available for instruction makes teaching anything more than the very basics impossible!

The amount of teaching time available is limited by the availability of a place to practice and the free time of the coaches, but another important limitation of how much you can teach is the interest span and retention rate of a 9- to 12-year-old child. If you expect him or her to absorb too much information and then recall it instantly in a game situation, you are being unrealistic. Considering all limitations, a coach is best advised to concentrate on the basics and drill them to the point that they become automatic in a game situation. As a child's baseball career continues, he or she can build on the foundation of those basics by gradually adding the finer points to his or her baseball knowledge and skills. Yet I never cease to be amazed at the number of Little Leaguers who have never even mastered the basics, e.g., hitting the ball and catching the ball, two skills that lend themselves so well to basic drills. Perhaps their coaches felt that they were *too* basic and that they should spend their teaching time on the more complicated aspects of the game.

Learning the basics is as much a mental process as it is a skill process, in my estimation. Yet how many managers you know hold "skull sessions" with their teams? I get my returning players together before the draft to discuss the scouting of prospects. At the same meeting, I start a series of skull sessions to review the mental basics with them, and then I continue those sessions when the new boys are added. (There's nothing better to do on a cold Sunday afternoon in March or on a rainout of a scheduled practice.) I apply the same philosophy to conducting these skull sessions as I recommend (in Chapter 8) for conducting an outdoor practice: keep it simple and make it fun!

I get the boys involved by asking them to explain plays or techniques, especially for the benefit of the new boys, using a drawing of a baseball diamond on a piece of paper and red and black checkers as players. (If you want to be fancy, make a felt board or a magnetic board.) I give them a written quiz at the end of each skull session, which keeps them on their toes during the session and adds a little competition to the practice. (See examples of the quizzes at the end of each of the next four chapters.) While they are having a Coke, I quickly score the quiz and give recognition to the winner, sometimes with an inexpensive prize, like some baseball cards or a wristband in our team's colors. After the boys have left, I analyze the quiz results to determine which questions were missed most, which tells me what I have to drill most heavily at the next session. The results of the skull sessions also indicate which boys have the most baseball savvy; they aren't always the boys with the best baseball ability. In a game that is going to be close, I want boys with baseball savvy as my base coaches, where a quick coaching decision could win a ball game!

The basics that I would drill, both in skull sessions and on the field, fall into five categories:

1. Rules
2. Hitting
3. Running the bases
4. Defense
5. Pitching

The next five chapters will cover these basics in the order listed above.

# 3
# DRILLING THE BASICS:
## THE RULES

There are 64 pages of fine print in the *Little League Baseball Official Regulations and Playing Rules* booklet. I attended Little League Umpires' School at Williamsport, Pennsylvania, where we took a two-hour written test on the rules after a week of both classroom and field instruction. There wasn't a perfect score in the group, and most of the men had been umpiring in Little League for some time. How much, then, can a manager be expected to teach a group of boys about the rules in the limited time available? Only the basics!

Several instructional aids on the rules are available, which your league may have in its library for your use. One is a booklet entitled *Official Little League Baseball Rules in Pictures;* the other is a set of slides that illustrates the rules. Both can be ordered from Little League headquarters, and both use clever cartoon illustrations to animate the rules.

For prices and ordering information on the book, the slides, or other instructional material available, I suggest you request a copy of the current *Little League Baseball Equipment and Supplies Catalog* by writing to Little League Baseball, Incorporated, P.O. Box 3485, Williamsport, PA 17701.

It is very important for managers, coaches, and umpires to have a working knowledge and understanding of the rules. Just reading the rule book and augmenting it with the aids mentioned above is not enough. A league should provide some preseason training for its managers, coaches, and umpires to make sure the rules are clearly understood and consistently interpreted. The first time our league did this, it improved the umpiring and the relations between managers/coaches and umpires. It is remarkable how many arguments can be avoided when all parties have been trained together!

It is also important to have refresher training and rule updating at the beginning of each season, even for those who have been trained and are experienced, since there are rule changes. We had an interesting case in point when an umpire made a ruling that would have been correct the previous year but had been unceremoniously changed. It was Rule 4.17, dealing with the forfeit of a game in progress when a team is unable or refuses to place 9 players on the field. In Chapter 9, I mention an incident involving a manager who consistently brought less than a full roster of players to a game, in this case only 11. Unfortunately, 3 of his players were hurt, so at the end of the third inning he could not field 9 players. The previous year, Rule 4.17 included a clause that said the game would be rescheduled in that situation, if it was not a regulation game (four innings completed). However, that clause had been deleted from the current year rule book, which meant the game was forfeited even though only three innings had been played. Unfortunately, the change had not been highlighted in our preseason training session, so the experienced umpire was calling it from past rulings. It was the only time I can recall that I ever won an argument with an umpire!

## IMPORTANT LITTLE LEAGUE RULES

As knowledgeable of the rules as managers, coaches, and umpires should be, it is not necessary (or practical) to drill your players on *all* of the rules. There are, however, some basics that should be drilled, since players could inadvertently violate certain rules if they aren't taught them. There are 20, in my estimation, that are important.

## 1. Mandatory Playing Rule

### *Regulation IV (i)*

Every player on a team roster will participate in each game for a minimum of six (6) defensive outs and bat at least one time.

*Penalty:* The player(s) involved shall start the next scheduled game and play no less than the mandatory time limit. The manager shall for the

A. First offense—receive a written warning.

B. Second offense—a suspension for next scheduled game.

C. Third offense—a suspension for remainder of the season.

*Note:* If the violation is determined to have been intentional, a more severe penalty may be assessed by the board of directors. However, forfeiture of a game may not be invoked.

### *Rule 3.03*

A player in the starting lineup who has been removed for a substitute may reenter the game once, in any position in the batting order, provided:

1. The substitute has completed one time at bat and;

2. Has played defensively for a minimum of six (6) consecutive outs.

3. A pitcher may not reenter the game as a pitcher.

4. Only a player in the starting lineup may reenter the game.

*Note:* (1) When two or more substitute players of the defensive team enter the game at the same time, the manager shall, immediately, before they take their positions as fielders, designate to the umpire-in-chief such players' positions in the team's batting order, and the umpire-in-chief shall notify the official scorer. The umpire-in-chief shall have the authority to designate the substitutes' places in the batting order, if this information is not immediately provided.

*Note:* (2) Should injury or illness prevent a manager from fielding nine (9) players, the manager may, without penalty of forfeiture, replace injured or ill players with a player previously in the lineup, but only if use of all other eligible players has exhausted the roster. This provision does not apply with respect to a player or players ejected from the game. If a team is unable to field nine

(9) players for reasons of ejection of a player, and no eligible substitute is available, previously used players may not enter the game.

*As will be mentioned in Chapter 9, "Letting Them All Play," it is important that the boys understand the mandatory playing rule and the reasons behind it: i.e., that every boy will get the opportunity to play in every game, but* how much *he plays will depend on his ability and hustle.*

*Each boy, especially a substitute, should be told to help keep track of his playing time in a game so his manager doesn't inadvertently try to take him out before he has played his six consecutive outs and batted at least once.*

## 2. Pitching Restrictions: Regulation VI

(a) Any player on a team roster may pitch.

(b) If a player pitches in less than four (4) innings, one calendar day of rest is mandatory. If a player pitches in four (4) or more innings, three (3) calendar days of rest must be observed. A player may pitch in a maximum of six (6) innings in a calendar week, Sunday through Saturday. Delivery of a single pitch constitutes having pitched in an inning.

Example:

| *If a player pitches in four or more innings on:* | *and is still eligible, that player can pitch again on:* |
|---|---|
| Sunday | Thursday |
| Monday | Friday |
| Tuesday | Saturday |
| Wednesday | Sunday |
| Thursday | Monday |
| Friday | Tuesday |
| Saturday | Wednesday |

(c) Only two players of league age 12 [league age refers to the age that a player will be before August 1st of the current year] may be used as pitchers during a calendar week. Either or both may pitch in one or more games, but each is limited to a total of six (6) innings within the calendar week and subject to rest periods described in section (b).

(d) A player once removed as a pitcher may not pitch again in the same game.

(e) Not more than five (5) pitchers per team shall be used in one game.

*Exception:* In case of injury to a fifth pitcher, an additional pitcher may be used.

(f) Violation of any section of this Regulation can result in protest of the game in which it occurs. Protest shall be made in accordance with Playing Rule 4.19.

*Note:* (1) The withdrawal of an ineligible pitcher after that pitcher is announced, but before a ball is pitched, shall not be considered a violation. Little League officials are urged to take precautions to prevent protests. When a protest situation is imminent, the potential offender should be notified immediately.

*Note:* (2) Innings pitched in games declared "no contest" or "Regulation Drawn Games" shall be charged against pitcher's eligibility for that week. If resumed in the following week or weeks, pitcher of record may continue up to six (6) innings or to the extent of remaining eligibility for calendar week.

*This regulation explains the rest requirements for each boy between pitching assignments, the maximum of six innings per week of pitching permitted, and the restriction against using more than two 12-year-old pitchers in a week. If your third-best pitcher is a third 12-year-old, he won't pitch much; but he needs to know that it is the rules, not his ability, that prevent him from pitching.*

## 3. Behavior toward Umpires and Other Team

### Rule 4.06

No manager, coach or player, shall at any time, whether from the bench or the playing field or elsewhere—

(1) Incite, or try to incite, by word or sign, a demonstration by spectators;

(2) Use language which will in any manner refer to or reflect upon opposing players, an umpire or spectators.

(3) In the umpire's judgment, any member of the offensive team makes any move calculated to cause the pitcher to commit a balk.

First warn the player and/or manager. If continued, remove the player and/or manager from the game or bench. If such action causes a balk, it shall be nullified.

(4) No fielder shall take a position in the batter's line of vision, with deliberate intent to distract the batter. The offender shall be removed from the game.

## Rule 4.07

When a manager, coach or player is ejected from a game, they shall leave the field immediately and take no further part in that game. They may not sit in the stands and may not be recalled.

## Rule 4.08

When the occupants of a player's bench show violent disapproval of an umpire's decision, the umpire shall first give warning that such disapproval shall cease. If such action continues—

*Penalty:* The umpire shall order the offender out of the game and away from the spectator's area. If the umpire is unable to detect the offender or offenders, the bench may be cleared of all players. The manager of the offending team shall have the privilege of recalling to the playing field only those players needed for substitution in the game.

*A manager's insistence on his players' strict compliance with this rule not only helps set a positive tone for a game but also helps prevent counterproductive distractions. Concentration is very important to a player's performance, so getting upset over an umpire's call or a rival player's taunts will serve only to break his concentration and impair his playing ability. Managers and coaches, of course, should be sure to set a good example in this regard.*

## 4. Use of Protective Equipment

## Rule 1.16

Each league shall provide in the dugout or bench of the offensive team seven (7) protective helmets which must meet Little League specifications and standards. Use of helmet by the batter, on-deck batter, all base runners and coaches is mandatory.

## Rule 1.17

All male players must wear athletic supporters. Catchers (male) must wear the metal, fibre or plastic cup type. Catchers must wear a mask during practice, pitcher warmup and games. Catchers must wear long-model chest protectors with neck collar, shin guards, and a catcher's helmet, all of which must meet Little League specifications and standards.

*Abiding by these rules will prevent painful injuries. Umpires will help to see that there is compliance in a game, but boys can get hurt just as easily in practice, and it is a temptation during practice sessions for a catcher to warm up a pitcher without his mask on or for a base runner to skip wearing a batting helmet. If you don't have a first aid kit, you'll need it. I also recommend a can of Cold Spray to help relieve the pain of bruises, particularly when a child gets hit with a pitched ball; it can be purchased in most sporting goods stores.*

## 5. Location of the Strike Zone: Rule 2.00 Definitions

The *strike zone* is that space over home plate which is between the batter's armpits and the top of the knees when the batter assumes a natural stance. The umpire shall determine the strike zone according to the batter's usual stance when that batter swings at a pitch.

*The strike zone is often erroneously defined as "shoulders to knees" or "letters to knees," when technically it is "armpits to knees." You should explain to your players that umpires, being human, do not always interpret the strike zone the same way; some seem to give the benefit of the doubt to the pitcher, others to the batter. If a particular umpire has a reputation for calling them close at the knees, tell your boys to expect it and not waste their time griping about it.*

## 6. Difference between a Foul Tip and a Foul Ball: Rule 2.00

A *foul ball* is a batted ball that settles on foul territory between home and first base, or between home and third base, or that bounds past first or third base on or over foul territory, or that first falls on foul territory beyond first or third base, or that while on or over foul territory, touches the person of an umpire or player, or any object foreign to the natural ground.

A *foul tip* is a batted ball that goes sharp and direct from the bat to the catcher's hands and is legally caught. It is not a foul tip unless caught and any foul tip that is caught is a strike, and the ball is in play. It is not a catch if it is a rebound, unless the ball has first touched the catcher's glove or hand.

*The basic difference is that the ball is live on a foul tip; e.g., a runner could steal on a foul tip but not on a foul ball. In fielding a foul ball, your infielders should know that a ball that rolls out of bounds along the first or third base lines could roll back across the line and end up being fair (e.g., because of the spin of the ball or by hitting a stone). Therefore, they should quickly field the ball while it is out of bounds. Conversely, a good bunt near the*

First baseman and catcher reach to touch the ball on foul side of line. Umpire will not call it foul until they do.

*baseline that the runner will probably beat out should not be touched in the hope that it will roll foul.*

## 7. Batter's Proper Position in the Batter's Box: Rule 6.03 and Definitions

The batter's legal position shall be both feet within the batter's box.

*Approved Ruling:* The lines defining the box are within the batter's box.

An *illegally batted ball* is one hit by the batter with one or both feet on the ground entirely outside the batter's box.

*The rules are clear, but often the lines of the batter's box are not. The most common infraction is called when a player steps on the plate when hitting the ball. If the lines of the batter's box are kept visible, the boys should understand that they must have both feet within the box when they hit the ball.*

## 8. Batter Hit by a Pitched Ball

### Rule 6.05

A batter is out when—

(f) That batter attempts to hit a third strike and is touched by the ball;

### Rule 6.08 (b)

The batter becomes a runner and is entitled to first base without liability to be put out when—

The batter is touched by a pitched ball which the batter is not attempting to hit *unless* (1) the ball is in the strike zone when it touches the batter, or (2) the batter makes no attempt to avoid being touched by the ball.

*Note:* If the ball is in the strike zone when it touches the batter, it shall be called a strike, whether or not the batter tries to avoid the ball. If the ball is outside the strike zone when it touches the batter, it shall be called a ball if that batter makes no attempt to avoid being touched.

Batter's stride has gone outside the batter's box. He is out *if he hits the ball.*

*Approved Ruling:* When the batter is touched by a pitched ball which does not entitle that batter to first base, the ball is dead and no runner may advance.

*It comes as a surprise to some to learn that a batter is not sent to first base every time he is hit by a pitched ball. He is not sent to first base if—*
*(a) he is hit while swinging at a strike;*
*(b) he is hit on a part of his body that is within the strike zone;*
*(c) he is hit by a ball that he makes no attempt to avoid.*
*We had a boy actually break a finger when the ball hit his hand while he was attempting to bunt. I had to control our fans, who were screaming at the umpire for not awarding him first base, by explaining to them that the umpire was right, as painful as the situation was for the boy.*

## 9. Batter or Runner Is Out when Hit by a Batted Ball before It Touches a Fielder

### Rule 6.05 (g)

A batter is out when a fair ball touches said batter before touching a fielder.

### Rule 7.08 (f)

Any runner is out when touched by a fair ball in fair territory before the ball has touched or passed an infielder. The ball is dead and no runner may score, no runners advance, except runners forced to advance.

*Exception:* If a runner is touching a base when touched by an Infield Fly, that runner is not out, although the batter is out.

*It may require some fancy footwork, but the runner or batter has to get out of the way of the ball. If it passes an infielder or ricochets off a fielder's glove and hits the runner, however, the batter is not out.*

## 10. Batter Is Out when Bunting Foul on a Third Strike: Rule 6.05 (d)

A batter is out when bunting foul on a third strike.

*This rule is sometimes misinterpreted to mean that you can't bunt on a third strike, and infielders almost always return to normal fielding positions after a bunter gets his second strike. With a boy at bat who is a poor hitter but a good bunter, I will sometimes give the bunt sign when he has two strikes, on the theory that a double play would be the worst thing that could happen and a probable strikeout would be no worse than a bunted foul. One of the batting basics I recommend drilling is bunting, so if you teach a boy how to bunt, you are sure to enjoy the tremendous satisfaction of seeing him bunt safely with two strikes on him. You might even be called a good coach when he does it.*

## 11. A Runner Interfering with a Thrown Ball or with a Fielder Attempting to Make a Play Is Out: Rule 7.08 (b)

Any runner is out when he intentionally interferes with a thrown ball; or hinders a fielder attempting to make a play on a batted ball.

*When a runner is hit on the back with a thrown ball, insult can be added to injury by his being called out, e.g., when he runs out a bunt inside the foul line on a direct line between the catcher throwing the ball and the first baseman attempting to catch it. That's why you should tell your players to run* outside *the baseline when running to first and from third to home.*

*If a base runner runs directly in front of a fielder attempting to field the ball, he could also be called out for interference. The runner must give the fielder clearance to field the ball.*

## 12. Obstruction by a Fielder: Rule 2.00 Definitions

*Obstruction* is the act of a fielder who, while not in possession of the ball and not in the act of fielding the ball, impedes the progress of any runner.

*In the preceding rule, we said a runner must give the fielder clearance to field the ball; the reverse is also true in the obstruction*

Runner from home to first should run outside of foul line. Runner is not interfering, and first baseman is not obstructing.

rule; i.e., the fielder, without the ball, must give clearance to the runner advancing to the next base. This rule frequently comes into play when a player is going from third base to home and the catcher is waiting for the throw. If the catcher blocks the base without the ball, he could be called for obstruction. The same could be true of any fielder without the ball who blocks the base or baseline from the runner.

### 13. Two Runners May Not Occupy the Same Base, and the Following Runner is Out when Tagged: Rule 7.03

Two runners may not occupy a base, but if, while the ball is alive, two runners are touching the base, the following runner shall be out when tagged. The preceding runner is entitled to the base.

*It happens! The key words are* when tagged, *so your players should be reminded that there is still hope when they find themselves in that embarrassing position. To play it safe, the leading runner should stay put and let the second runner worry about getting back to the previous base without being tagged. The lead runner could do a little decoying to distract the fielders if his teammate is in a rundown between bases. A trapped runner should always try to force as many throws as possible, since each additional throw creates the chance of a wild throw.*

## 14. Tagging Up on a Fair or Foul Ball Caught: Rule 7.08 (d)

Any runner is out when failing to retouch the base after a fair or foul fly ball is legally caught before that runner or the base is tagged by a fielder. The runner shall not be called out for failure to retouch the base after the first following pitch, or any play or attempted play. This is an appeal play.

*You should teach your base coaches to do their job in this situation. A base coach should act like the starter in a race ("ready, get set, go!") in telling a base runner to leave the instant the ball hits the fielder's glove. Hand signals can be used by the third base coach for the runner on second. The coach must judge whether or not the runner can make it, but if the runner has to hesitate in*

Catcher has the ball and can block the plate. Runner must slide to avoid the tag.

*making the decision, looking in one direction and running in another without help from the coach, he may lose the one step that would be the difference between being safe and being out. From both offensive and defensive standpoints, your players should realize that a runner may tag up and advance (at his peril) on a* foul *fly ball that is caught. For example, with a runner on second and a foul fly ball hit to the third baseman deep behind third base, and no one covering third, the runner would have a good opportunity to advance to third after the catch.*

## 15. Force Play and Removal of Force: Rule 7.08 (e)

Any runner is out by failing to reach the next base before a fielder tags said runner or the base, after that runner has been forced to advance by reason of the batter becoming a runner. However, if a following runner is put out on a force play, the force is removed and the runner must be tagged to be put out.

*Young ball players easily understand the concept of a force play, yet frequently in a game situation they will be confused, both as infielders and as runners, about whether or not a tag is necessary. The best coaching advice to a runner is "When in doubt, slide"; and to a fielder, "When in doubt, tag." Both would be good advice when there is a question as to whether the force has been removed. For instance, on a ground ball to the first baseman, with a man on first, did the first baseman touch first before throwing to second? Sometimes neither the runner, with his back to the play, nor the shortstop, whose view is blocked by the runner, can see what the first baseman did.*

## 16. When and How Appeals Should Be Made: Rule 7.10

Any runner shall be called out on appeal when:
(a) after a fly ball is caught, the runner fails to retouch the base before said runner or the base is tagged;
(b) with the ball in play, while advancing or returning to a base,

the runner fails to touch each base in order before said runner, or a missed base, is tagged;

*Approved Ruling:* (1) No runner may return to touch a missed base after a following runner has scored. (2) When the ball is dead, no runner may return to touch a missed base or one abandoned after said runner has advanced to and touched a base beyond the missed base.

(c) the runner overruns or overslides first base and fails to return to the base immediately, and said runner or the base is tagged;

(d) the runner fails to touch home base and makes no attempt to return to that base, and home base is tagged.

Any appeal under this rule must be made before the next pitch or any play or attempted play. If the violation occurs during a play that ends a half-inning, the appeal must be made before the defensive team leaves the field. (The defensive team has left the field when no players remain in fair territory.)

An appeal is not to be interpreted as a play or an attempted play. Successive appeals may not be made on a runner at the same base. If the defensive team on its first appeal errs, a request for a second appeal on the same runner at the same base shall not be allowed by the umpire. (Intended meaning of the word *err* is that the defensive team, in making an appeal, threw the ball out of play. For example, if the pitcher threw to first base to appeal and threw the ball into the stands, no second appeal would be allowed.)

*I know of no other sport in which a player can break a rule in full view of an official (umpire) but have the official take no action unless the other team sees the infraction and complains, and then only if the other team follows the proper procedure for complaining! Don't blame this strange rule on Little League; it's in the rules of all organized baseball, starting with the Major Leagues. It was applied in a World Series game several years ago, when a runner on third base tagged up on a fly ball, but in full view of the third base umpire left the base before the ball was caught, and scored. The umpire did nothing until the catcher returned the ball to the pitcher, and the pitcher, before throwing another pitch, threw the ball to the third baseman, who touched third and said to the umpire, "I appeal; the runner left third base too soon." Only then did the umpire call the runner out. The appeal would not have been allowed if time had been called, or if the pitcher had thrown wild to third base, or if the third baseman had merely touched third but failed to announce his appeal verbally. It seems like a cumbersome way to enforce a rule, but that's the way it is written.*

*The two most frequently appealed plays are a runner's missing a base and a runner's tagging up and starting to the next base before the ball is caught. The error most frequently made in appealing a play involves calling time. The ball must be live for an appeal to be legal; even on a home run hit out of the park, when the runner fails to touch a base, a legal appeal cannot be made until the umpire puts a new ball in play. And to make the situation even more complicated, you get only one chance at an appeal on a play; if you goof—e.g., making an appeal when the ball is dead— you don't get another chance when the ball becomes live again.*

*A personal example will attest to the vagaries of the rule. One of our runners failed to touch home plate, and our on-deck batter yelled out to him to come back. Hearing this, the pitcher called for a time-out and threw the ball to the catcher. The catcher appealed, and the umpire called our runner out. I protested on the basis that the pitcher had called time and the ball was dead. The umpire acknowledged that the pitcher had asked for a time-out but reminded me that only the umpire can call time out! We had insult added to injury; if our own player had not called attention to the missed base, the appeal might not have been made, and if the umpire had granted the time-out requested by the pitcher, the appeal would have been illegal.*

*You should point out to your players the four situations in which an appeal should be made:*

1. *A base runner misses a base.*
2. *A man on base leaves for the next base before a fly ball is caught.*
3. *A man fails to return to base after a fly ball is caught before he or the base is tagged;*
4. *A runner fails to touch home plate.*

*You should point out that the important thing in an appeal situation is to* act quietly first *and appeal verbally second. In other words, a fielder should either touch the base or tag the runner and then make his verbal appeal to the umpire. If his first reaction is to start shouting, "He missed second base," calling the runner's attention to that fact, too, the runner may beat the ball back to second. And under no circumstances should he (or you) call time out!*

## 17. Infield Fly Rule: Rule 2.00

An *infield fly* is a fair fly ball (not including a line drive or an attempted bunt) that can be caught by an infielder with ordinary effort, when first and second or first, second and third bases are occupied, before two players are out. The pitcher, catcher and any outfielder stationed in the infield on the play shall be considered infielders for the purpose of this rule.

When it seems apparent that a batted ball will be an infield fly, the umpire shall immediately declare, "infield fly," for the benefit of the runners. If the ball is near the baseline, the umpire shall declare, "infield fly, if fair."

The ball is alive, and runners may advance at the risk of the ball being caught, or retouch and advance after the ball is touched, the same as on any fly ball. If the hit becomes a foul ball, it is treated the same as any foul.

*Note:* If a declared infield fly is allowed to fall untouched to the ground and bounces foul before passing first or third base, it is a foul ball. If a declared infield fly falls untouched to the ground outside the baseline and bounces fair before passing first or third base, it is an infield fly.

*Young players have no trouble understanding the concept of and reason behind the infield fly rule, but they do have trouble remembering the situations to which it applies. I tell them to try to remember it as the "first and second fly rule," since it always applies with runners on first and second bases. Whether third base is occupied or not doesn't matter. The other thing they need to understand is that, if the umpire shouts, "Infield fly rule!" when the ball is in the air, as he should, he isn't "blowing the play dead." The ball is live, and a play can be made on a runner if he is off the base, or the runner can advance to the next base if the ball is not caught—or after the ball is caught—if he can make it without being tagged out.*

## 18. Overrunning First Base: Rule 7.08 (c)

Any runner is out when that runner is tagged, when the ball is alive, while off a base.

*Exception:* A batter-runner cannot be tagged out after overrunning or oversliding first base if said batter-runner returns immediately to the base.

*You would think this is too basic to have to emphasize, but a surprising number of young players instinctively slow down as they near first base. That slowing down can make the difference between being safe and being out on a close play. I drill my boys on running to first like it is a 20-yard dash and time them with a stopwatch in practice to emphasize the importance of treating first base like the finish line of a race—which you run over. A myth regarding first base is that you can be thrown out if you turn toward the infield on returning to first. The rule says the batter-runner cannot be tagged out after overrunning first base if he immediately returns to the base. It doesn't matter which way he turns back, toward the infield or away from it, as long as he returns immediately.*

## 19. Runner Leaving Base Too Soon: Rule 7.13

When a pitcher is in contact with the pitcher's plate and in possession of the ball and the catcher is in the catcher's box ready to receive delivery of the ball, base runners shall not leave their bases until the ball has been delivered and has reached the batter.

*This rule is unique to Little League baseball, resulting from the fact that leading off base is not permitted. The rule takes up nearly two pages of small print in the rule book, most of it concerning the action taken by the umpire when the rule is violated in every conceivable game situation. You should not confuse your players by trying to explain the various ramifications of the rule, since even you and the umpires will have trouble remembering them and, when the need arises, will probably resort to checking the rule book. (No good manager, coach, or umpire should be without one.)*
*Your boys need only understand the basic fact that they cannot leave the base until the ball has reached the batter. What they must also understand is that they will not be called out if they leave base too soon; the worst penalty is having to return to the base. Many young players mistakenly think that they risk being called out for*

*leaving the base too soon. Consequently, they become very timid about leaving the base at all until the ball is hit.*

*We tell our boys to get a head start of at least two steps off the base on every pitch as it reaches the plate*—especially if they are in a force play situation. *Even if a runner would leave first base too soon in an attempted force play at second—and beat the throw to second*—he would not be penalized; *both runners would be safe, and the fact that the runner on first left too soon would be academic, in complete compliance with the rule. That is why you should urge your players to get a good start off the base in a force play situation, even at the risk of leaving too soon.*

## 20. Pitching Positions and Balks

### Rule 2.00

A *balk* is an illegal act by the pitcher with a runner or runners on base, entitling all runners to advance one base.

### Rule 8.01

*Legal pitching delivery.* There are two legal pitching positions, the windup position and the set position, and either position may be used at any time.

(a) *The windup position.* The pitcher shall stand facing the batter, the entire pivot foot on or in front of and touching and not off the end of the pitcher's plate and the other foot free. From this position any natural movement associated with the delivery of the ball to the batter commits the pitcher to pitch without interruption or alternation. The pitcher shall not raise either foot from the ground, except that in the actual delivery of the ball to the batter, said pitcher may take one step backward and one step forward with the free foot.

*Note:* When a pitcher holds the ball with both hands in front of the body, with the entire pivot foot on or in front of and touching but not off the end of the pitcher's plate and the other foot free, that pitcher will be considered to be in a windup position.

(b) *The set position.* Set position shall be indicated by the pitcher when that pitcher stands facing the batter with the entire pivot on or in front of, in contact with, and not off the end of the pitcher's plate, and the other foot in front of the pitcher's plate, holding the ball in both hands in front of the body. From such set position the pitcher may deliver the ball to the batter, throw to a base, or step backward off the pitcher's plate with the pivot foot. Before assuming set position, the pitcher may elect to make any natural preliminary motion such as that known as the *stretch*. But if the pitcher so elects, that pitcher shall come to set position before delivering the ball to that batter.

*Note:* The pitcher need not come to a complete stop.

## Rule 8.05

If there is a runner or runners, a balk occurs when:

(a) the pitcher, while touching the plate, makes any motion naturally associated with the pitch and fails to make such delivery;

(b) the pitcher, while touching the plate, feints a throw to first base and fails to complete the throw;

(c) the pitcher, while touching the plate, fails to step directly toward a base before throwing to that base;

(d) the pitcher, while touching the plate, throws or feints a throw to an unoccupied base, except for the purpose of making a play;

(e) the pitcher makes an illegal pitch;

(f) the pitcher delivers the ball to the batter while not facing the batter;

(g) the pitcher makes any motion naturally associated with the pitch while not touching the pitcher's plate;

(h) the pitcher unnecessarily delays the game;

(i) the pitcher, without having the ball, stands on or astride the pitcher's plate or while off the plate feints a pitch;

(j) (not applicable in Little League);

(k) the pitcher, while touching the plate, accidentally or intentionally drops the ball;

(l) the pitcher, while giving an intentional base on balls, pitches when the catcher is not in the catcher's box.

*Penalty:* The ball is dead, and each runner shall advance one base without liability to be put out, unless the batter reaches first base on a hit, an error, a base on balls, a hit batter, or otherwise, and all other runners advance at least one base, in which case the play proceeds without reference to the balk. When a balk is called, if the pitch is delivered, it will be considered neither a ball nor a strike unless the pitch is ball four (4), awarding the batter first base and forcing all runners on base to advance.

*Approved Ruling:* In cases in which a pitcher balks and throws wild, either to a base or to home plate, a runner or runners may advance beyond the base to which they are entitled at their own risk.

*Approved Ruling:* A runner who misses the first base to which that runner is advancing and who is called out on appeal shall be considered as having advanced one base for the purpose of this rule.

*Rule 20 applies to pitchers, and once you have settled on who your pitchers will be, you would be well advised to drill them on the foot positions on the rubber, for both the windup and set positions; on developing a pitching rhythm; and on understanding the rules concerning balks.*

*In addition to the normal balks, there are some careless balks that catchers, as well as pitchers, should understand because a catcher sometimes causes them in making a poor return throw to the pitcher:*

1. *A pitcher accidentally drops the ball while toeing the rubber.*
2. *A pitcher puts his foot on the rubber before he has the ball.*
3. *A catcher goes outside the catcher's box to receive a pitch on an intentional walk.*

The foregoing are the 20 rules that I would recommend you emphasize to your team in both skull sessions and practice drills. Not to diminish the importance of the several hundred additional rules and regulations covered in the 64 pages of the official rule book, I think that these 20 will suffice for the attention span of a 9- to 12-year-old. The rest can be left to their managers and coaches to digest and understand.

As mentioned in the introduction of this chapter, we have developed a quiz for each of the following basics we teach: rules, hitting, running the bases, defense, and pitching. We give these quizzes after a skull session on each of the basics. The purpose is as much to measure what we have taught (and need to teach more of) as to measure what the boys have learned. Recognition should be given to the boy who scores highest, but, to avoid embarrassment to the slow learner, the rest of the scores should not be made public. We let the players score their own quizzes, which provides an additional opportunity to drill the rules as we review the quizzes and discuss the right and wrong answers. Sometimes I will give each player an additional copy of the quiz to take home and give to his or her dad or older brother. We hope the player will at least read it again as another teaching drill. On the following pages is the quiz on basic rules, with a key to the correct answers at the end.

## LITTLE LEAGUE BASEBALL QUIZ: RULES

Circle Correct Answer
*True*     or     *False*

| | True | False |
|---|---|---|
| 1. Batter is out if he hits the ball with one foot outside the batter's box. | T | F |
| 2. Batter swings at third strike but is hit by the pitch, so batter goes to first. | T | F |
| 3. A batter can bunt on the third strike. | T | F |
| 4. A batter can be called out if he bunts down the first baseline, running inside of it, and is hit by the thrown ball from the catcher to the first baseman. | T | F |
| 5. A substitute player must remain in the game until he has batted at least once and played at least six consecutive outs on defense. | T | F |

6. If two base runners end up on second base, . . . both runners are out.  T      F

7. . . . the second runner is automatically out.  T      F

8. . . . the second runner has to be tagged out.  T      F

9. A base runner is out if hit by a batted ball before a fielder has an opportunity to touch it.  T      F

10. A base runner is out if hit by a batted ball after it touches a fielder's glove.  T      F

11. A team may not pitch three 12-year-old boys in the same week.  T      F

12. If a pitcher pitches four innings on Monday, he can still pitch two innings on Wednesday.  T      F

13. According to the *infield fly rule*, the batter is automatically out if he hits an infield fly ball . . . with two outs and runners on first and second.  T      F

14. . . . with one out and runners on first and third.  T      F

15. . . . with no outs and the bases loaded.  T      F

16. . . . with one out and runners on first and second.  T      F

17. If a bunt rolls just over the third base foul line, the third baseman should wait to see if it rolls back into fair territory before touching it.  T      F

18. With a runner trying to score from third, the catcher should block the plate while he waits for the throw.                    T          F

19. A man is on base, and the pitcher, with his foot on the pitching rubber, accidentally drops the ball. This is a balk.          T          F

20. With a runner on base, it is a balk when the pitcher, without having the ball, stands on the pitching rubber.                  T          F

21. When a pitcher is in contact with the pitching rubber and the catcher is in the catcher's box, ready to receive the ball, base runners may not leave their bases until the ball has reached the batter.                     T          F

22. If a base runner leaves the base too soon, he is automatically out.                   T          F

23. A base runner on second leaves too soon, and the batter hits a single. The runner must return to second.                        T          F

24. A base runner leaves first too soon. The batter hits a grounder to the shortstop, who tries to get the force play at second, but the runner from first beats the throw. The runner has to go back to first because he left too soon.              T          F

25. A batted ball that hits fair but rolls foul after it passes third base is a foul ball.                       T          F

26. A runner may tag up and advance after a foul fly ball is caught.　　　　T　　　　F

27. It is legal for a runner to run into a fielder fielding a ground ball if the fielder is within the baseline.　　　　T　　　　F

28. Base runners should always sprint off base at least two steps every time the ball reaches the batter.　　　　T　　　　F

29. There is a runner on third base, and the batter hits a fly ball that is caught, but the runner tags up and leaves third base before the ball is caught and scores; . . . the runner is automatically out.　　　　T　　　　F

30. . . . the run counts if the defensive team does not appeal to the umpire.　　　　T　　　　F

31. . . . the defensive team must touch third base with the ball and then appeal to the umpire to have the runner called out.　　　　T　　　　F

32. If a batter hits a triple, but fails to touch second base, . . . he is immediately called out if the umpire sees that he failed to touch second.　　　　T　　　　F

33. . . . he is out only if the defensive team throws the ball to second base and appeals to the umpire.　　　　T　　　　F

34. Any pitch that is over the plate and between the knees and the armpits of the batter is a strike.　　　　T　　　　F

35. When in doubt as to whether to tag the runner, a baseman should tag the runner and the base.  T          F

36. When the batter hits an infield ground ball, he should slow up as he reaches first base to avoid overrunning it.  T          F

37. When in doubt as to whether to slide, the runner should always slide.  T          F

---

PRINT NAME                    DATE       SCORE

## ANSWER KEY

| | | | |
|---|---|---|---|
| 1. T | 11. T | 21. T | 31. T |
| 2. F | 12. F | 22. F | 32. F |
| 3. T | 13. F | 23. T | 33. T |
| 4. T | 14. F | 24. F | 34. T |
| 5. T | 15. T | 25. F | 35. T |
| 6. F | 16. T | 26. T | 36. F |
| 7. F | 17. F | 27. F | 37. T |
| 8. T | 18. F | 28. T | |
| 9. T | 19. T | 29. F | |
| 10. F | 20. T | 30. T | |

# 4
# DRILLING THE BASICS:
## HITTING

During my 15 years of coaching in Little League, I have often wondered why so few boys hit the ball so few times. The strikeout rate in Little League baseball is awful! It is not unusual for more than half of the outs in a game to be strikeouts, and, sadly, it is not unusual for a boy to go through an entire season hardly ever laying a bat on a ball. I'm not referring to base hits, but *just to hitting the ball!*

I wish I could attribute the universally poor hitting to universally superior pitching—a good mixture of fastballs, curveballs, sliders, and knuckleballs—but the fact is that most Little League pitchers throw nothing but a fastball (and some aren't all that fast). Typically, the good Little League pitchers have a fastball and control; that means they throw more balls in the strike zone for the batters to hit. Why, then, don't they hit more? I think it is because *we don't teach and drill the basics of hitting.*

One of the problems in teaching hitting may lie in refining the skill of hitting to such a few fundamentals that 9- to 12-year-old youngsters can remember them. Consider the number of different things we ask young Little Leaguers to remember when they come to bat. The Little League official *Training and Instructional*

*Handbook,* an excellent teaching manual, lists no fewer than 11:

1. Always keep eyes on the ball.
2. Swing a bat that can be controlled.
3. Step as far back in the batter's box as possible.
4. Spread feet at a comfortable distance.
5. Keep front arm away from the body.
6. Keep bat back and still.
7. Hold hands chest high and in front of the rear shoulder.
8. Swing level and keep hips and shoulders level.
9. Take a short stride; don't lunge.
10. Follow through.
11. Choke your bat.

Walter Alston and Don Weiskopf, in their comprehensive book, *The Complete Baseball Handbook,* concur on those 11 and add 5 more:

12. Have a positive attitude.
13. Keep front shoulder in.
14. Keep your head down.
15. Don't hitch with your hands.
16. Anchor your rear foot.

If we add bunting (which, after all, *is* also hitting), the two manuals add 12 more things to remember! Can you believe that, in the process of coaching rookies on how to bat, we should teach them 28 different things to remember? If you told *them* that, they would certainly agree with the premise that baseball is a complicated game!

Adults learning the game of golf frequently complain about the number of things *they* have to remember when swinging a club (arm straight, head down, follow through, etc.). Rookie Little Leaguers would consider the golf swing easy to master, compared to the baseball swing, since not only do golfers have fewer things to remember, but they can also take their time in remembering them before they swing. Rookie ball players, however, have to remember their 28 points in the split second between the time the ball leaves the pitcher's hand and the time it reaches the plate.

All of the instruction manuals make a common error in teaching hitting: they make it appear to be a science. That is, they imply that there are specific things a batter must do in certain precise ways to be a good hitter. If hitting was a science, then shouldn't you expect every good hitter to do it in the same way, with the same stance, same stride, same position of the hands, etc.? The manuals then contradict themselves with descriptions and pictures of the *different ways successful hitters bat!* The fact is that every successful hitter follows only a few basic hitting principles; the rest comes from the style and rhythm that become a comfortable and automatic system for the player. Teaching Little Leaguers a few basic batting principles, and then drilling them so they develop a style and rhythm that are comfortable and automatic for them are precisely the same objectives that I recommend.

To simplify the skill of batting, I recommend dividing the fundamentals into the two broad categories of on-deck and at-bat basics. If the batter is able to make some decisions while he is in the on-deck circle, then he has less to think about when he gets up to bat.

## ON-DECK BASICS

1. Select your bat.
2. Practice your swing.
3. Decide on batting box position.
4. Adopt a positive attitude.

### Select Your Bat

There is a popular myth among Little Leaguers that the bigger the bat, the better the batter. Our smallest rookie received a 31-inch bat as a birthday present and proudly brought it to practice. (If only his parents had asked!) His correct bat size was 27 inches, so I had to suggest that he put his birthday present away for at least several years. Few Little League hitters show the symptoms of using too light a bat—e.g., swinging early or consistently fouling down the third baseline (for a right-handed batter)—but many show the symptoms of using a bat that is too heavy, such as swinging late or consistently fouling down the first baseline (for a right-handed batter). In my experience, there are very few Little Leaguer hitters who should use anything larger than a 28-inch bat. What young batters need to understand is that *bat speed, not bat size,* is important in hitting the ball. It stands to reason that a light bat is faster and easier for a youngster to control than a heavy one.

One bad habit of Little Leaguers is experimenting with different bats after the season starts. All a player has to do is bring a shiny new bat to a game and, regardless of its size or weight, everyone wants to try it. The players have to be reminded that every "big leaguer" uses one personal bat and sticks with it, and so should they. Experimentation should be done in early season practice, and, with the help of the coach, each player should settle on the bat that he can swing the fastest and control the best. And then he should stick with it. The more he uses it, the more comfortable he will become with it and the better he will be able to control it.

## Practice Your Swing

Controlling a bat, like controlling a hammer, is done more easily when the bat is choked. (Did you ever try hitting a nail by holding a hammer at the very end of the handle?)

While in the on-deck circle, the batter should be practicing his stride and swing. He may find it helpful to use the "doughnut" (weight) for several swings to limber up his arms and shoulders. Then I recommend that he practice his timing by watching the pitcher and swinging his bat when the boy at bat is swinging his. By studying the pitcher, he can familiarize himself with his motion, check when and where the ball is first visible, and estimate the speed of the ball. He should be active and moving in the on-deck circle; otherwise he will start to tense up as his time at bat approaches.

## Decide on Batting Box Position

While in the on-deck circle, the next batter should be deciding where he will stand in the batter's box. Some training manuals advocate having a Little Leaguer stand as far back in the batter's box as possible, for two good reasons: (1) It gives the batter the longest possible time to watch the ball. (2) It makes the catcher move back, which requires him to make a longer throw on a steal and to move forward a greater distance on a bunt.

I believe that is good advice when the batter is facing a good fastball pitcher and has the sign to swing away. If he has been

On-deck batter practices his timing by watching the pitcher and swinging his bat as the boy at bat swings his.

given the sign to bunt, however, he should stand forward in the batter's box to bunt the ball before it reaches the plate. If the pitcher is slow, his pitches will tend to arc down over the plate, and the batter should move forward in the box. I have seen many good fastball hitters get totally frustrated when the opposing team puts in a slow pitcher and they can't adjust. One of the adjustments that they should make, in my opinion, is to move forward in the batter's box so that they can get out in front of the ball and hit it before it starts to arc downward. When the next batter is in the on-deck circle, he should be deciding—with some help from his coach— where he should stand. The coach should remind him of the decision as he leaves the circle but shouldn't be surprised if he forgets in the time it takes him to walk from the on-deck circle to the plate. Such is often the memory span of a Little Leaguer under pressure. If the player does forget, the coach should call time out, meet the batter down the line, and, without chewing him out for forgetting, just quietly tell him again where to stand in the batter's box.

## Develop a Positive Attitude

This is the most important of the on-deck basics. When the batter leaves that circle and heads for the plate he has to believe in himself; *he has to believe that he is going to hit the ball.* We often see young players step up to the plate, convinced that they are going to strike out (it is evident in every move they make), and prove that they were right by striking out. The opposite is just as obvious; cocky players who walk up to the plate looking like hitters (this is just as evident in every move *they* make) prove *they* are right by either hitting the ball or so intimidating the pitcher that they get a walk. The poem says it best:

If you think you are beaten, you are.
If you think you dare not, you don't.
If you'd like to win, but think you can't,
It's almost a cinch you won't.
Life's battles don't always go
To the stronger or faster man;
But soon or late the man who wins
Is the one who thinks he can.

A player must believe he *can* hit. If one of our players needs his confidence reinforced, I ask him as he leaves the on-deck circle, "What are you going to do, Joey?" The response he knows I want to hear is "I'm going to *hit that ball!*" By saying it enough, he starts to believe it, but how he says it really tells how positive his attitude is. Admittedly it's a gimmick, but if it serves to help convince a young player that *he can do it*, it is a well-conceived gimmick.

## AT-BAT BASICS

It is interesting to note that none of the instructional manuals even touches on one of the most basic fundamentals that I believe must be dealt with early in teaching a young boy how to hit: overcoming the fear of being hit by a pitched ball. It will happen sooner or later, and he knows it. There is no point in telling him it won't hurt, because it *does* hurt, and he knows that, too. As long as he is concentrating on that fear when he is at bat, you can be sure he won't be thinking about the batting tips he is supposed to remember.

We had a big, physically strong 12-year-old pitcher several years ago who could throw a blazing fastball. In the first game of the season, he hit in the side a boy whose reflexes should have been quick enough to prevent him from being hit but weren't because he was a rookie in his first Little League game. Fortunately, the boy wasn't hurt, but he was inclined to overdramatize things, so you would have thought he was in mortal pain to watch him moaning and writhing on the ground. After his coach finally got him quieted down and on first base, and the umpire called for the next batter, the coach found he had another problem. The next batter, also a rookie, after watching the scene that had just transpired, retreated to the farthest corner of the dugout and refused to come out!

I have seen boys get physically ill and others develop painful symptoms as manifestations of fear and pressure. One of my boys needed only to be told that he was going into the lineup, and he turned pale and complained of stomach cramps. Unfortunately, he had been hit painfully by pitched balls several times before the episodes began. His parents took him to their doctor, who found no physical reasons and had to conclude that the symptoms were psychosomatic, caused by fear of getting hit again.

Every coach is familiar with the first sign of a scared batter; he "steps in the bucket" (steps backward with his back foot), preparing to "bail out" if any pitch looks like it might come inside. This boy was particularly likely to step in the bucket because of his acute fear. To help him overcome the problem, we drilled him in bunting, theorizing that the concentration required to follow the ball in for an attempted bunt would take his mind off his fear. Accidentally, we discovered that it had another good effect since the position of the feet for a bunt makes stepping in the bucket virtually impossible. Ironically, not only did the bunting drills help him regain his confidence and virtually eliminate his fear, but he also became the best bunter on the team! We found something that he could do well, which did more than anything else to restore his confidence.

The accidental discovery that bunting drills will help a young player overcome his fear of getting hit led us to two important training conclusions: (1) The number one basic fundamental of at-bat hitting should be *concentration*. (2) The way to teach it is with bunting drills. In other words, contrary to the normal training sequence of teaching hitting first, then bunting, we teach bunting first because we think it helps players develop the first basic in hitting: concentration. Have you ever noticed how often a player will bunt foul and then, with the bunt sign off, get a solid hit? We observed how often it happened, and it reinforced our belief that bunting will sharpen a young player's concentration in judging the pitched ball.

Concentration goes beyond watching the pitch. It requires a total mental commitment to watching the ball that blocks all other thoughts from the mind. We hear sports commentators refer to something "breaking the concentration" of an athlete, usually in the context of poor performance. Because of their age, Little Leaguers do not have a great concentration span to begin with, so it is a real challenge for a coach to drill into their heads the importance of *total concentration.* "It's just you and the ball," I tell them. "Get mad at it, go after it, and block out all other sounds or thoughts." Youngsters are easily bothered and distracted by what opposing players and fans might yell at them when they are up at the plate, and even though that is contrary to Little League rules, it happens. The purpose of such barbs is obviously to distract the batter and make him think about something other than hitting the ball; in short, to "break his concentration."

## Batting Signs

Ironically, a batter's coach and/or teammates can be guilty of breaking his concentration at bat, inadvertently, by shouting instructions from the bench. When the hitter leaves the on-deck circle to concentrate on hitting the ball, he should be left alone, without friendly advice distracting him any more than unfriendly barbs. Occasionally, batting signs from the coach will be necessary, but they should be so few and so uncomplicated that they will not risk breaking his concentration. I recommend only three signs: hit, take (don't swing), and bunt. Normally, these signs will be given only in special situations; e.g., the take or hit sign will be given when the count is 2 and 0, 3 and 0, or 3 and 1. As a standard rule, your players should be told to fake a bunt (and fake it early) when they are given the take sign. Little League pitchers seem to have trouble pitching to hitters in the bunt position, so the batter has a good chance of coaxing another ball. You have to caution the batter when he fakes a bunt to pull back before the pitch reaches the plate so the umpire will not rule that he was going for the pitch

Author's son Jim checks the sign before stepping into the batter's box.

and call it a strike. If you want a boy to bunt, tell him so before he leaves the on-deck circle and remind him to check the sign before each subsequent pitch.

I have tried to add the hit and run sign but found that the boys were confused by the fact that they were expected to do one thing on the hit sign and something different on the hit and run sign, i.e., to swing only if the ball is in the strike zone on the former, but to swing wherever the pitch is on the hit and run sign. You could almost read the batter's confused thoughts—"Do I *have* to swing or not?"—and the hit and run sign served only to break his concentration. Or if the batter did get the right sign, the runner often would not, and you would have a "busted play" anyway. It just got too far away from the basics!

The signs themselves should be brief and direct so that there is no opportunity for confusion. I clap my hands for the hit sign, touch my cap for a bunt, and put my hands together in a fake bunt position for the take sign, which also reminds them to fake bunt. It isn't necessary to use any more complicated signs because there is very little sign stealing in Little League. If you think the other team is paying attention to your signs, then give a series of five signs and tell your players which sign is the right one; e.g., "the third sign is the one you should follow." So long as you don't change the number too often, your players will be able to handle that routine. Caution them, however, to watch the full sequence of five signs before stepping back in the batter's box, since looking away after the third sign will tip off the other team which is the key sign.

## The Three At-Bat Basics

In addition to concentration, we added just two other at-bat basics so the young hitters would have only three things to remember when they come to the plate:
1. concentration
2. arms back and ready
3. stride/swing

To make it easy for them to remember those three things, I drew an analogy between hitting and hunting:

| HITTING | HUNTING |
|---|---|
| Concentrate on the pitched ball. | Sight on the target. |
| Arms back and ready. | Cock the gun. |
| Stride/swing (one coordinated motion). | Pull the trigger. |

A batter has to develop a batting rhythm that becomes automatic. Analyzed in the training manuals, it is the process of putting the weight back on the rear foot and then bringing it forward as the front foot strides and the arms, wrists, and bat thrust against a stiff front leg. That becomes too complicated to explain to rookies, but they *can* remember the analogy of shooting a gun. We tell the rookie he's a pheasant hunter who has to make a split-second decision as to whether his target is a hen or a cock pheasant (a ball or a strike) before shooting. The preparation is the same in either case; he has to sight on the target, cock the gun, and either fire or pull back at the last instant. He cocks his gun by bringing his arms back, and, when he does that, his weight will automatically shift back to his rear foot. Then he starts shifting his

Little League coach Floyd Friend checks the correct batting stance of his son J.R.

weight forward with his stride and completes it with the forward thrust of the bat. His weight will shift properly without his realizing it or even having to think about it.

Developing a comfortable rhythm is a personal skill for each Little Leaguer, just as it is for each big leaguer. When it is right, he (and you) will know it, and then it becomes a matter of drilling to make it automatic. Just as a young player tends to use a bat that is too heavy, there is a tendency for him to rear back and lunge at the ball. (He's going to kill it but good!) Overswinging and/or overstriding will affect his timing or will destroy his rhythm. The arms should go back about the same distance that the stride goes forward, which helps maintain a balance that is important to the rhythm. For Little Leaguers, it should not be more than six inches in either case.

Your players should be urged to start practicing their stride and swing when they are in the on-deck circle and to continue it when they get up to the plate—before the first pitch and between pitches. I remind them that a statue has no rhythm and can't hit a baseball, and if they stand up at the plate like a statue, they won't hit a baseball either. I also suggest that they count the number of practice swings most big leaguers take when they are at bat the next time they watch a game on TV. When I recently took two of my sons to Pittsburgh to see a Pittsburgh Pirates' game, we watched Pete Rose at bat. He was never still until the pitcher started to deliver the pitch; between pitches, he was out of the batter's box and then back in again when *he* was ready; he took practice swings after every pitch, as many as he could take (I counted as many as six between two pitches). He was staying loose, keeping his rhythm going until the moment he started sighting on the ball. He was the complete opposite of the frozen statue, which characterizes too many of our Little Leaguers. Pete Rose looks and acts like he is going to hit the ball, and his credentials as a hitter speak for themselves.

## Bunting

To complete the basics of hitting, we should cover the basics of bunting. As mentioned earlier, we feel bunting should be taught early in the batting training of a young player, since it helps him develop that all-important first basic of hitting: concentration. It also helps him overcome the fear of being hit by a pitched ball.

Too little bunting is done in Little League games because it isn't taught and drilled. Yet simple logic should encourage a coach to teach his young boys how to bunt, if not for the two reasons given above, then for these additional reasons:

1. It is easier to bunt than to hit.

2. Little League pitchers seem to have trouble pitching in the strike zone to a batter assuming the bunt position.
3. If the batter does bunt the ball in fair territory, he has a good chance of making it to first, especially if he catches the defense by surprise.

I remind my players that there is only one thing they can do at bat that will make it impossible for them to have a chance to get on base, and that is striking out. Even a poorly hit bunt is better than a strikeout because the batter still has four chances of making it to first: he may beat the throw; the infielder may "boot" the ball (commit an error); the infielder may throw wild to first; and/or the first baseman may drop the ball!

The training manuals, written for experienced players, make bunting seem so complicated that Little League coaches are discouraged from teaching it and young players from learning it. They list these 12 things a batter should remember in a sacrifice bunt:

1. Grip bat lightly.
2. Square feet (or pivot).
3. Keep eyes on the ball.
4. Crouch body slightly.
5. Bend knees slightly.
6. Keep arms relaxed in front of body.
7. Slide top hand up and cup the bat.
8. Hold bat parallel to the ground.
9. Start bat at top of strike zone and come down.
10. Don't jab at ball.
11. Catch ball on fat end of bat.
12. Bunt only good pitches.

These 12 points don't even cover the techniques of the drag or push bunt. I don't talk drag bunt or push bunt to my players; the distinction made in the manuals between a sacrifice bunt and bunting for a base hit is semiacademic for the average Little Leaguer. We are accomplishing a lot if we can just teach a boy the basics of how to bunt a ball in fair territory because, in most cases in Little League play, any bunted ball will be bunted for a base hit, whether there is a man on base or not.

The first two basics of bunting are the same as in hitting, so bunting is merely substituting a different movement for the third step in hitting and doing it at the last moment to ensure the surprise element. For stride/swing (the third basic in hitting), we substitute "square/crouch." Thus, the three basics of bunting are:

1. concentration
2. arms back and ready
3. square/crouch

## Foot Position

The manuals cover the two foot positions in bunting: squaring around versus pivoting in your tracks. The latter has the theoretical advantage of allowing the batter to wait longer before tipping off the infield that he is bunting. That advantage is not as significant in Little League as it is at higher levels of play, and it is more difficult to teach a Little Leaguer to pivot. If you have a player square around with both feet pointing toward the pitcher, the batter can more easily see that his bat position is proper, i.e., in front of the plate, level, and in the top of the strike zone.

## Hand Position

Positioning the hands sometimes causes problems for young players. The textbook description of hand position calls for the player to slide the top hand up, keeping fingers underneath and thumb on top, with the thumb and index finger forming a *V.* Try explaining that to a young Little Leaguer, and be sure to add the caution about getting his fingers smashed, and I guarantee that you will discourage him from bunting. The problem with the textbook description is that it was written for long-armed adults, not short-armed children. Trying to hold the bat with the bottom hand at the end of the bat and the upper hand three-quarters of the way up the bat is just plain awkward for a short-armed Little Leaguer. He can't control the bat and move it quickly, which is essential in bunting.

To make it simple and easy to understand, we teach the beginner merely to relax his grip on the bat as both hands, held apart, slide up the bat. He then lets the ball hit the bat *above* his hands, which is the fat part of the bat. The finer points of bunting technique can

Both hands slide up the bat, and batter lets the ball hit the bat above his hands as he bunts the ball.

be taught in drills as the young batter masters the basics. Bunting should be included as an integral part of the hitting drills, which follow. In the final chapter, "Winning," bunting will be discussed as a strong offensive weapon in a versatile winning strategy.

So much for defining the basics of hitting. Knowing them and doing them are two different things, however, and drilling is what makes them the same.

Chapter 8, "Practice: Keep It Simple, Make It Fun," outlines six hitting drills—from individual to team practice. To drill the mental part of hitting, give your boys the following quiz during a skull session when practice is rained out. Hope that all of your boys score well; that will mean you have scored well as a coach in teaching and drilling the basics of hitting.

## LITTLE LEAGUE BASEBALL QUIZ: BATTING

Circle Correct Answer
*True* or *False*

1. If you are the batter, facing a hard-throwing but wild pitcher, you should keep thinking about how to avoid being hit by a pitched ball.     T        F

2. A light bat is harder to control than a heavy one.     T        F

3. The batter should look for the take sign . . . when the count is 3 and 0.     T        F

4. . . . when the count is 0 and 2.     T        F

5. . . . when the count is 3 and 2.     T        F

6. . . . when the count is 3 and 1.     T        F

7. . . . when the count is 2 and 2.     T        F

8. . . . when the count is 2 and 0.     T        F

9. . . . when the count is 1 and 2.     T        F

10. If you are convinced you can't get a hit off a good pitcher, you should wait for a walk.     T        F

11. If you get the take sign, you should fake a bunt and fake it early.     T        F

12. To check the sign after the batter is in the batter's box, the batter must ask the umpire to call time and step out of the batter's box.     T        F

13. When the count is 3 and 0 on you, you can anticipate that the pitcher will try to throw a strike right down the middle.     T        F

14. If the coach gives you the hit sign on a 3 and 0 count, it means you *have* to swing at the next pitch.                    T            F

15. If the batter doesn't understand the sign the coach gave him, he should just do whatever he thinks is right.          T            F

16. If you go up to the plate afraid you will strike out, you probably will.                        T            F

17. A batter who is afraid of being hit by a pitched ball will probably be a good hitter.          T            F

18. Always hold the bat in front of the plate when bunting.          T            F

19. If the first and third basemen are playing deep, you should never bunt.                          T            F

20. A left-handed batter has a better chance of bunting than a right-handed batter because he is a step closer to first base.   T            F

21. You should hold your bat low when bunting because it is easier to raise the bat if the ball is high than to lower it if the ball is low.                      T            F

22. Face the pitcher as the ball comes in when you're bunting.       T            F

23. If the coach signals you to bunt, you *have* to bunt at the ball, whether or not it is in the strike zone.                     T            F

24. When you are in the on-deck
    circle, don't do anything but
    rest before you go to bat.                T              F

25. The bigger the bat, the better
    the batter.                               T              F

26. Facing a slow pitcher, you
    should probably stand in the
    front part of the batter's box so
    you can hit the ball before it
    starts to arc downward.                   T              F

27. If you are right-handed and hit
    a lot of fouls down the first
    base foul line, it may mean . . .
    you have too heavy a bat.                 T              F

28. . . . you are swinging too late.          T              F

29. . . . you are swinging too soon.          T              F

30. If you are a right-handed
    batter and hit a lot of fouls
    down the third base foul line, it
    may mean . . . you have too
    light a bat.                              T              F

31. . . . you are swinging too late.          T              F

32. . . . you are swinging too soon.          T              F

33. When at bat, follow the ball
    from the pitcher's hand into
    the catcher's mitt.                       T              F

34. Most Little League batters
    should use a light bat and
    choke it.                                 T              F

35. Standing back in the batter's
    box gives you longer to watch
    the pitch coming in.                      T              F

36. With a man on base, the batter can make it more difficult for the catcher to throw to second by standing back in the batter's box.  T  F

37. Every Major League baseball player bats the same way, and so should you.  T  F

38. You should practice your swing and batting rhythm while you are in the on-deck circle.  T  F

39. A good hitter can concentrate hard enough to see the stitches on the ball as it comes into the plate.  T  F

40. As a batter, never move your feet once the pitch is thrown.  T  F

41. Each time you go to bat you should be confident that you will hit the ball.  T  F

42. If a player on the other team yells something at you when you are at bat, keep trying to concentrate on what he called you so you can get even when he is up at bat.  T  F

43. If your coach tells you to bunt before you go up to the plate, you don't have to check for any more signs after the first pitch.  T  F

44. Once you are in the batter's box, you cannot take any more practice swings.  T  F

45. If you act like a hitter when you go to the plate, it will affect the way the pitcher throws to you.　　　　T　　　　F

46. If you act timid and afraid of being hit when batting, it will affect the way the pitcher throws to you.　　　　T　　　　F

47. You don't have to stride if the pitch is a ball.　　　　T　　　　F

Fill in Correct Answer

48. What is the first at-bat basic of hitting? _____

49. What is the second at-bat basic of hitting? _____

50. What is the third at-bat basic of hitting? _____

51. What is the first basic of bunting? _____

52. What is the second basic of bunting? _____

53. What is the third basic of bunting? _____

54. All you need is a ball and a bat, and you can practice hitting and bunting by yourself.　　　　T　　　　F

## ANSWER KEY

| | | | | |
|---|---|---|---|---|
| 1. F | 12. T | 23. F | 34. T | 45. T |
| 2. F | 13. T | 24. F | 35. T | 46. T |
| 3. T | 14. F | 25. F | 36. T | 47. F |
| 4. F | 15. F | 26. T | 37. F | 48. Concentration |
| 5. F | 16. T | 27. T | 38. T | 49. Arms back and ready |
| 6. T | 17. F | 28. T | 39. T | 50. Stride/swing |
| 7. F | 18. T | 29. F | 40. F | 51. Concentration |
| 8. T | 19. F | 30. T | 41. T | 52. Arms back and ready |
| 9. F | 20. T | 31. F | 42. F | 53. Square/crouch |
| 10. F | 21. F | 32. T | 43. F | 54. T |
| 11. T | 22. T | 33. T | 44. F | |

# 5

# DRILLING THE BASICS:
## BASE RUNNING

You can almost see a Little Leaguer relax when he gets on base. The tension of being a hitter is over as he reaches that safe haven: a base. But therein lies one of the problems in teaching Little Leaguers proper base running. You will first notice it in a practice drill of running from home to first. Invariably a rookie will slow up as he reaches first and will avoid overrunning the base as if his life depended on it. "A base is safety, so get to it and cling to it," seems to be his goal. You expect this of a rookie at his first practice. But when you see it with a team at mid-season, you know the coach has not drilled the basics of base running.

The other mistake a rookie makes in running from home to first on a batted ball is watching the ball. I try to instill in my players the fact that the run from home to first base is a 20-yard foot race. If they were running a 20-yard dash in track, where would their eyes be? On the finish line, of course. Would they slow up as they reached the finish line? Of course not. They would put on a final burst to cross the finish line *at full speed*. That technique of running from home to first will spell the difference between being safe and being out on many close plays at first. Overcoming the feeling that a base is a safe haven, to be reached and not left, will

The run from home to first base is a 20-yard foot race!

come only with drilling the basics of running to first base. To stress the analogy of a foot race, I conduct foot race drills between home and first in every practice session, periodically timing them on a stopwatch to encourage them to improve their speed until they subconsciously view that 20-yard stretch as a racetrack.

To emphasize the point, I take a page out of Pete Rose's book and drill my boys in *running to first even when they get a walk*. "What do you do when you get a walk?" I ask. "You run!" they answer. If "Charlie Hustle" can do it, they can do it, and it will not only reinforce the importance of hustling to first but will also get a savvy runner to second base on a walk when he sees that the catcher and/or pitcher is not watching him and that no one is covering second base. He just takes off from home and doesn't stop until he gets to second. The element of surprise will upset the concentration of the other team, particularly the pitcher, who has compounded the error of issuing a walk by letting the runner go to second. We so frustrated one team with this aggressive base running that the opposing manager ordered his catcher to call time out every time one of our boys got a walk, only to be more frustrated by the umpire, who would not grant time out until the play was completed, i.e., when the runner showed no inclination to go beyond first base. Most Little League players are too tentative, play it too safe, in base running, so when an opposing team has to encounter an aggressive base runner, they get unnerved.

One myth that has endured over the years is that a runner who overruns first base can be thrown out if he turns toward second. As pointed out in the chapter on rules, this is not true. A base runner, overrunning first, must make an overt move toward second base to be vulnerable.

Reluctance to give up the safe haven of a base is also a problem in teaching inexperienced boys to get a fast start toward the next base. I encourage them to take a stance on their toes, facing home plate, and to spring off the base two steps *every time* the pitched ball reaches the plate. Two steps is not far enough to get picked off by a good catcher, but it is two steps closer to the next base if the ball gets through the catcher or is hit. Some boys are afraid of leaving base too soon and, as a result, do not leave soon enough. I would rather have an aggressive runner err in the direction of leaving base too soon than be caught flat-footed by leaving too late, particularly since the penalty for leaving too soon is so mild. You need to emphasize that a player is not out for leaving the base too soon; he merely has to return to the base he left early—*but only if that base is not occupied.* As pointed out in the chapter on

Runner is ready to push off first base as he follows the pitch into the plate.

rules, if a runner on first leaves the base too soon and reaches second on a ground ball, with the batter reaching first base safely, there is no penalty. Even if the umpire saw the runner leave first early and dropped a flag on him, he could not send him back to first base since it would now be occupied by the batter. So, obviously, being an aggressive runner is worth the risk of leaving the base too soon.

Aggressive base running is a case not so much of being a fast runner as of being a *smart* runner or, more accurately, a well-coached runner. The only way your boys will learn to be smart runners is by your drilling them on the basics, the right moves in basic base running situations—both in skull sessions and in simulated game situations in practice. Use runners in conjunction with other drill practices, such as batting practice or infield fielding practice. You will provide the opportunity to teach both skills at the same time.

Since we emphasize basics, we don't recommend complex running plays like hit and run, hit behind the runner, suicide bunts, etc. You will just be frustrated by lack of recall on the part of your players on the rare occasions that such complex plays would be called. I recommend the following 10 basic rules of base running and drill them in skull sessions and practice.

*1. Run on anything with two outs.* That is probably the most familiar base running rule, but you have to teach a rookie *when* to run, namely, at the "crack of the bat." In a close game, we had two outs with a rookie on second, representing the tying run, and a runner on first. The batter hit a fly ball to left field, which the outfielder dropped. You can understand my frustration when I looked out and saw the rookie still standing on second base. The left fielder picked up the ball and threw it to third base for a force play on the rookie, and instead of having a tie game with only two outs, we were still a run behind with three outs. You and your base coaches should remind rookie runners to "run on anything" as often as possible (even before every pitch!).

*2. Run on a ground ball whenever you're forced.* If a runner hesitates, he just gives the infielders an easy force out on what could have been a close play.

*3. Jump off the base two steps on every pitch.* If it's a fly, come back and tag up; on a wild pitch, steal; on a hit, keep moving. The important thing is to make the base runners keep on their toes, and drilling this rule will help.

*4. Home to first is a foot race.* We've already covered this. Challenge your boys to think of the exception that proves this rule. For example, if the first baseman has to field a slow roller and elects to tag out the runner rather than make the play at first, the runner should slide into first to avoid the tag rather than run into the tag.

*5. On a hit, always take a turn toward the next base.* This is another instance in which you have to overcome the "safe haven" attitude of boys who are so relieved that they got to the base that they just stop there.

*6. When you get a walk, run to first!* We've also covered this. I believe in doing anything and everything to avoid an easy force play, and this is one that will work surprisingly often. For instance, the runner will be able to keep going to second when he sees that whoever has the ball is not looking and second base is not covered.

*7. When in doubt about whether to slide or not, slide!* Even on "sure out" force plays, the slide will break the concentration of the infielder and often cause errors.

*8. Don't take chances with no outs or two outs.* Trying to stretch a double into a triple could stop a potential rally when there is no one out, and it could end a rally and the inning when there are two outs.

*9. With runners on first and third and fewer than two outs, the runner on first should steal second on the first pitch to the next batter.* In most cases, he could walk to second and the catcher won't make a play on him. The runner on third, in this situation, needs to be cautioned not to be fooled by a fake play to second, where the shortstop or pitcher can cut off the ball and relay it back to the catcher to nail the runner coming home.

*10.    A runner on third base should be ready to steal home when the ball gets past the catcher and the pitcher fails to cover home.* In addition to this obvious opportunity to score, the runner should watch for another, less obvious situation. A frequent mistake a Little League catcher will make on a passed ball that doesn't go too far is to retrieve the ball and throw it back to the pitcher from the spot where he retrieves it, instead of running back to home plate first. A runner on third, two steps off the bag, can normally beat the throw to the plate if he takes off for home when the catcher throws the ball back to the pitcher. The pitcher not only has to catch the ball thrown by the catcher, but he has to throw it back to the catcher running back to home plate from wherever he retrieved the ball. Add to that the advantage of the element of surprise, and you usually will have a run scored.

To help remind runners to be smart, you must train smart base coaches. Although you can do some coaching from the dugout, try coaching a runner coming into third base when you are in the first base dugout. You need a third base coach with savvy to tell your runner whether to slide, hold up, or keep going home. The rules require that you use players rather than adults as base coaches. Some managers treat them as honorary positions or, worse yet, just don't have base coaches. The boys enjoy being base coaches, and with some drilling you can teach them how to help your players be smart runners. There are three obvious signs that they should be taught to use when coaching a player coming into the base they are coaching:

1. *Keep going.* This is a windmill circle with the right arm. We tell boys not to watch the ball when they are running the bases; they should be looking to the base coach for a sign.
2. *Hold up.* Holding both hands up to stop is the best sign. It tells a runner that he can make the base standing up but should stop there.
3. *Slide.* The base coach should crouch with the palms of his hands close to the ground.

You should teach your on-deck batter to be the base coach for a runner trying to score. Your base coaches should be urged to exaggerate the signs so there can be no mistaking them. Timid

Three base coaches demonstrate the three coaching signs (left to right): windmill means "keep going," hands down means "slide," hands up means "stop."

signs are almost as bad as no signs at all.

A base coach has some other important functions that must be drilled:

1. He should remind a runner of the number of outs *before every pitch.* You can't do this too often. The traditional hand signals of no outs (fist); one out (index finger); and two outs (index and little finger) should be used by the third base coach to signal to a runner on second.
2. He should remind the runner if there are other runners on base. There is nothing so embarrassing to a runner on first than to steal second, only to find a teammate already there.
3. He should remind the runner of any other applicable base running rules, e.g., "Run on anything," "Run on a ground ball," etc.

The third base coach position is the more important of the two, and you should schedule your most savvy team member to fill this position. You can often use the scores on skull session quizzes to identify boys who have the most baseball savvy. You will be

Third base coach reminds runners on second and third that there are "two outs; run on anything."

surprised to find that some of your boys who are not physically your best players are mentally your best and therefore would make good base coaches.

Earlier in this chapter, I recommended using base runners in conjunction with batting and/or fielding drills so that you can drill both skills. At the same time, you can use base coaches in order to drill them on the things they should do in game situations. Boys will get bored in practice if they are substitutes and not included in a drill. By using them as base runners and base coaches, and rotating them with the regulars in hitting or fielding, you can prevent boredom, and you will be getting the most mileage out of your practice sessions because you can be drilling hitting, fielding, base running, and base coaching all at the same time. You should also add situation drills in the base running that will add fun to practice, while sharpening their skills. One that they will enjoy is the "hot box" (i.e., a runner trapped in a rundown between bases) drill. The runner should be taught these basics in the drill:

1. Never turn your back on the ball.
2. Change directions frequently.
3. Force as many throws as possible.
4. Given a choice, try to reach the farthest base.
5. Slide to avoid a tag.

More will be said about this in Chapter 8, "Practice: Make It Simple, Keep It Fun."

The following quiz will help you evaluate how good a base running coach you have been.

This base coach's "hand on hip, finger in your ear, and spit" sign was strictly ad lib.

## LITTLE LEAGUE BASEBALL QUIZ: RUNNING THE BASES

Circle Correct Answer
*True*     or     *False*

1. If you get a walk, you should run to first base to show the other team you are anxious to run the bases on them.     T          F

2. If you hit a single to the outfield, you can relax in running to first base, knowing you will make it easily.     T          F

3. If you hit a ground ball to the infield, you should race to first base like it is a 20-yard dash and overrun the base.     T          F

4. On a hit to the outfield, you should take a good turn at first, looking for an extra base if possible.     T          F

5. In rounding first base, touch the inside corner of the base, pushing off the base to give you a strong start toward second.     T          F

6. In running from first to second base, you could be called for interference if you run in front of the second baseman as he is preparing to field the ball.     T          F

7. After you hit the ball, you should always watch where it is going as you run to first.     T          F

8. Many hitters are thrown out at first by one step, which is why speed is necessary if you are going to be a good ball player.     T          F

9. Batters should run to first base
   slightly outside the base line.    T          F

10. If you hit a fly ball to an
    outfielder, you should slow up
    as you round first base to see
    if he catches the ball.    T          F

11. On most fly balls to the
    outfield that an outfielder
    drops, the batter should easily
    reach second base if he is
    hustling.    T          F

12. In running to first, the batter
    should watch the first base
    coach and not the ball.    T          F

13. In going into second base, you
    should always slide if the play
    may be close.    T          F

14. If there is any doubt about
    whether you should slide or
    not, slide.    T          F

15. There is no point in sliding
    into second base if the umpire
    has called you out on a force
    play.    T          F

16. In going into third base, you
    should watch for the coach's
    signal to decide whether to
    slide, stand up but stop, or
    keep going home.    T          F

17. If you are going into third base
    and the third base coach is
    crouched with his hands close
    to the ground, that is the sign
    to keep going home.    T          F

18. If you are rounding third base
   and coming home, and the on-
   deck batter gives you no sign,
   you can assume it is safe to go
   into home standing up.          T         F

19. If you are on second and the
   batter gets a hit to the outfield,
   you should watch the third
   base coach and not the ball.      T         F

20. Runners on first and second
   must run to the next base on a
   ground ball.                        T         F

21. You are the third base coach.
   Your team has a man on first
   with no one out and the score
   tied. The hitter gets a double,
   and the runner from first might
   be able to score. Since the run
   would put your team ahead,
   you should give him the sign
   to try to score.                  T         F

22. You are the third base coach.
   You have a fast runner on first
   base with two outs in the
   bottom of the last inning with
   the score tied. There is a good
   hitter up, followed by a weak
   hitter. The good hitter gets a
   clean double, and you think
   the runner from first has a
   chance to score, so you should
   give him the sign to keep
   going home.                    T        F

23. You are the third base coach. It
   is the first inning, with no
   score and no outs. The batter
   hits a double, and the fielder
   fumbles the ball, so the batter

continues around second and
looks to you for a sign. You
think he has a 50/50 chance of
making it, so you should signal
him to run to third and slide.          T                F

24. Aggressive base runners often
force errors by the opponents.           T                F

25. When you are a base runner
you should fake a steal on
every pitch, running toward
the next base a few steps
every time the ball crosses the
plate.                                   T                F

26. It is poor sportsmanship to
steal second when you see the
opposing team put in a
substitute catcher or second
baseman.                                 T                F

27. Early in the season, you can
take more chances stealing
because the opposing team's
catcher and second baseman
are inexperienced.                       T                F

28. If you are a runner on first
base, you should leave the
base and head for second
when you see the ball get
through the catcher.                     T                F

29. It is poor sportsmanship to
rattle the pitcher and catcher
by always faking runs to the
next base.                               T                F

30. The base runner should check
the opposing team's lineup to
see if there is a substitute
catcher or a substitute fielder
covering the next base.                  T                F

31. You should watch how opposing outfielders field balls hit to them to know which ones you can run on.                T                    F

32. If you are on first and the ball is hit to right or center field, you should be able to make it to third base.                T                    F

33. If you are on second, no one is on first, and the ball is hit on the ground to the shortstop, you should break for third so the shortstop will look at you and miss the ball.                T                    F

34. If you are on first and the batter hits an easy ground ball to the second baseman, who tags second base, you may as well stop running and get off the field.                T                    F

35. If you are a runner trapped between two bases, never turn your back on the ball.                T                    F

36. If you are a runner trapped between bases, quick changes of direction may help you get free.                T                    F

37. If you are a runner trapped between bases, try to force as few throws as possible.                T                    F

38. If you are a runner trapped between bases, never slide to avoid being tagged, since it takes more time.                T                    F

39. Since most teams put in their substitutes in the third and

fourth innings, you can take
more chances in running the
bases in those innings.                    T            F

40. If you are running from third
base to home, you should run
on the foul territory side of the
third baseline.                            T            F

41. If you overrun first base, and
the shortstop throws wild over
the first baseman's head, you
have to go back and touch first
base before going on to
second.                                    T            F

42. If you overrun third base, the
runner ahead of you is trapped
between third and home, and
you want to go back to second
base, you must retouch third
base before going back to
second.                                    T            F

_____   _____   _____
PRINT NAME                        DATE        SCORE

**ANSWER KEY**

| | | | | |
|---|---|---|---|---|
| 1. T | 10. F | 19. T | 28. T | 37. F |
| 2. F | 11. T | 20. T | 29. F | 38. F |
| 3. T | 12. T | 21. F | 30. T | 39. T |
| 4. T | 13. T | 22. T | 31. T | 40. T |
| 5. T | 14. T | 23. F | 32. T | 41. F |
| 6. T | 15. F | 24. T | 33. F | 42. T |
| 7. F | 16. T | 25. T | 34. F | |
| 8. T | 17. F | 26. F | 35. T | |
| 9. T | 18. F | 27. T | 36. T | |

# 6
# DRILLING THE BASICS:
## DEFENSE

Does it seem too obvious to say that the basics of defense are throwing and catching a baseball? If you think so, then wait until the first time you have to coach a boy who doesn't know how to throw and/or catch a ball. You will then come to marvel at the number of *experienced* Little Leaguers who have never been taught the basics of how to throw and/or catch a baseball, which is all the more surprising when you realize that they are skills that can easily be taught by drilling the basics.

## THROWING TECHNIQUE

It is easy to spot a boy who doesn't know how to throw. He either throws with an awkward, off-balance throw, caused by throwing off the wrong foot, or he throws weakly, which is caused by throwing off neither foot. There is an analogy between throwing and batting. In both cases, you are coming forward with your strong arm and stepping forward with your opposite foot at the same time. A right-handed boy will come forward with his right hand over his shoulder, at the same time stepping toward his target with his left foot and following through with his throwing arm.

In both hitting and pitching, you come forward with your strong arm and step forward with your opposite foot.

## Playing Catch

Since playing catch is an age-old drill that requires only two children and a ball and can be played anywhere, it is even more surprising that there are so many players who can't throw properly. It must be because no one has ever corrected their faulty throwing, so every game of catch merely compounds a poor technique. Since playing catch should be the initial drill of every practice in order to limber up the players' arms, a coach should easily be able to spot a boy who is not throwing properly. To teach him the right way, I position him behind one of the best throwing boys and have him go through the motions of the boy in front of him until the motion becomes automatic. Then it will require drilling the basics until the wrong motion is forgotten and the correct motion is established as automatic.

The "playing catch" drill can start as soon as the first boy shows up for practice by having the coach participate until others arrive. The boys should start throwing to each other about 20 feet apart, gradually increasing the distance to 60 feet (the distance between bases). Once the throwing arm is limbered up, accuracy in throwing should be stressed, with the bull's-eye being between the waist and the shoulders of the catcher. In Chapter 8, the "Five and Ten" game is explained, which makes playing catch a competitive game between two players, sharpening their throwing accuracy.

## CATCHING TECHNIQUE

Catching is the other basic skill that can be improved only with frequent practice, but the proper way to catch must be taught first. One of the most frequent, and most obvious, mistakes an inexperienced player will make is turning his head as the ball gets close. It is an instinctive fear of the ball that causes it, but unfortunately, turning the head will cause more injuries than it will prevent, and this must be emphasized to your players. If a boy doesn't want to get hit with the ball—whether catching a throw, a ground ball, or a fly ball—he should never turn his head because that causes him to take his eyes off the ball. As long as he keeps his eyes on the ball, his reflexes will help him avoid a ball that might hit him. But if he takes his eyes off the ball by turning his head, a ball that curves or is deflected may hit him. So, as in batting, fear of getting hit by the ball is a condition that coaches must deal with in working with young, inexperienced players.

## FIELDING GROUND BALLS

Fielding a ground ball is another basic skill that will become automatic with practice drills. Fear of getting hit by the ball is also a problem with this skill, and it must be overcome if a boy is to become a good infielder. The three symptoms of this problem are (1) turning the head, (2) straightening up when fielding a grounder, and (3) "side saddling" a ground ball (fielding the ball to the side,

Infielders and outfielders must be down, ready, and on their toes.

instead of in front, of his body). The proper stance for an infielder is crouched, butt down, hands down and in front, back parallel to the ground, weight on the toes. It is a position that must be drilled, and the coach should be watching for the lazy infielder who relaxes his position and is not ready to react to a ground ball. Young boys have a short concentration span, and it is natural in a slow-paced game for an infielder to relax and sit back on his heels or rise out of the crouched position. I watch for it and shout, "Fielding position, Charlie!" when I see a boy relaxing to remind him to be on his toes (literally) and ready for an infield play.

In addition to drilling the fielding stance, the other basics of fielding a ground ball can be described best by two familiar rules:

1. Play the ball; don't let it play you.
2. Look the ball into your glove.

In the first instance, it is important that a boy be ready to move instantly to intercept the ball rather than sit back on his heels and wait for the ball to come to him. That's why fielding stance, with the player's weight on his toes, ready to move, is important. A rolling ball will stick in a fielder's glove better when that glove is coming forward to scoop it; a bouncing ball is more difficult to field, and judgment on whether to field it on the big hop or the short hop will come only with the experience of participating in a lot of grounder drills.

"Looking the ball into your glove" is a way of reminding an infielder to keep his eye on the ball all the way. If he looks the ball into his glove, he won't make the mistake of coming up too soon and suffering the embarrassment of seeing the ball go under his glove. A boy cannot look the ball into his glove and at the same

Chuck Tanner checks correct infield position of Little Leaguer J. R. Friend.

time turn his head or rise for fear of getting hit. If you can get him to master the skill of looking the ball into his glove, at the same time you will have helped him overcome the natural fear of getting hit by a ground ball, and you will have yourself a promising infielder. It is gratifying to a coach, after hitting hundreds of ground balls to an infielder, to see him handle the play routinely, moving to the ball, keeping down, pulling it into his glove, and in a fluid motion making the throw to first. It will happen, but only after the basics have been drilled and a lot of ground balls have been fielded in practice. A practice routine that keeps two ground balls in play simultaneously is outlined in Chapter 8. It allows your coaches to hit several hundred ground balls in each practice session, with each additional ground ball handled bringing your infielders closer to the point at which fluid-motion fielding becomes routine.

## CATCHING FLY BALLS

Catching fly balls is another basic drill that will show remarkable improvement with practice drills. Each year I am pleasantly surprised, and always gratified, to see a boy who couldn't come close to catching a fly ball in preseason practice catch fly balls routinely by mid-season. But a lot of fly balls were hit to him in the interim. It is an indictment of the coaching staff when a rookie doesn't even attempt to catch a fly ball in a Little League game. It tells the world that his coaches haven't spent much time drilling the basics.

The safest and best way to teach a boy to catch a fly ball is with the two-handed, over-the-head catch. One-handed catches and basket catches, if taught at all, belong in advanced-level play. The primary skill of judging a fly ball and getting into a position to catch it comes only after many fly balls have been hit, or thrown, to a player.

One technique I have found to be helpful is to have the boy point to the ball with his throwing hand as soon as it is in the air. "Sighting on the ball" is a little like sighting on an object with a camera and bringing it into focus. It is a good technique for an infielder to use on a pop fly ball, too, because it not only helps him judge the position of the ball but also lets the other fielders know that he plans to catch it. The two-handed catch is the safest, surest catch, and it puts a boy's throwing hand on the ball, ready for the throw-in when there are runners on base.

One of the most boring and inefficient practice drills, but one you see quite often with Little League teams, is a coach hitting fly balls to a group of disorganized boys. Only the boy who catches the ball is active, and he risks straining his arm if he has to throw the ball all the way back to the coach. When we drill the basics of catching fly balls we combine it with drilling the basics of throwing

Center fielder has made two-handed catch, and right hand is ready for the relay throw. Note right fielder has moved over to back up.

to the relay man and then having the relay man pivot and throw to the catcher. So, instead of one drill, we combine it with two others and keep three boys involved with each fly ball that is hit in practice. To make it a fun, competitive drill, we even have a way of keeping score for each team of three, so they can compete with the other teams of three involved in the drill. (This drill is described in detail in Chapter 8.)

Coach Harold O'Dell keeps three boys active by hitting fly ball to outfielder, who throws to relay man, who throws to catcher. Boys rotate positions and compete with other three-member teams by scoring three points for a catch and one point for good throws and catches to relay man and catcher.

## DEFENSIVE STRATEGY

If you have done a good job of teaching your boys the basics of throwing a ball, catching a ball, fielding a grounder, catching a fly ball, and making an accurate throw after the catch, and have spent the requisite time in drilling those basics until they become automatic, then you have done a fine job of coaching. With a good command of those basic skills and an understanding of the basics of defensive strategy, your boys will do you proud in the field. Defensive strategy, as it is employed in the Major Leagues, can be very complicated. But remember that you are a part-time coach, working with part-time child-players and a limited practice schedule. All you can hope to accomplish in teaching defensive strategy, as with everything else we have covered, is the basics. The following are the basics of defensive strategy that I have found Little Leaguers can handle without getting confused. Since they involve thinking, as well as doing, they need to be drilled in skull sessions and reinforced in simulated game situations.

*1. Every fielder should have a backup.* In every defensive play, each player involved in the play should be backed up by another player. For example, on an infield ground ball, the player fielding the ball should be backed up by another infielder and/or an outfielder, and the first baseman taking the throw should be backed up, also by another infielder and the right fielder.

Every fielder should have a backup. Here second baseman has backed up shortstop, who has taken the throw on a steal.

An outfielder catching a fly ball should be backed up by the closest other outfielder. In a rundown play, both infielders who have the runner trapped should be backed up by two other infielders.

The relay man, receiving the throw from an outfielder, should be backed up by another infielder. An infielder taking a throw to a base should be backed up by another infielder. The pitcher should back up the third baseman or catcher on any throw to either of those bases. On an attempted steal, the second baseman should back up the shortstop, or vice versa, and the center fielder should back up both.

As part of your skull sessions, describe situations and ask your boys who the backup player should be. Once they have the fact drilled in their minds that every fielder should have a backup fielder, and they receive enough practice in simulated game situations to understand this basic defensive rule, making the proper backup move in a game will become instinctive.

*2. Cover the ball or a base.* On every batted ball, especially with runners on base, each defensive player should go toward either the ball or a base at the crack of the bat. For example, with a runner on first and an extra base hit to right field:

- right fielder fields the ball and throws to the relay man;
- center fielder moves toward the ball to back up the right fielder;
- second baseman moves toward the ball to take the relay;
- first baseman covers first base;
- shortstop covers second base, also backing up the relay man;
- third baseman covers third base;
- left fielder backs up third base;
- pitcher goes between third and home and backs up the base where the ball is thrown;
- catcher covers home.

I realize that, in Major League play, with this example, the first baseman would move to the center of the infield to be the cutoff man, but I have found that cutoff strategy is too complicated for Little Leaguers to understand. In addition, the Little League infield is so much smaller than a regulation baseball diamond that a cutoff man is not necessary and only gets in the way of the other infielders. If the catcher realizes the throw to the plate is going to be too late, he can step forward to take the throw high and act as the cutoff man, if a play at second or third is possible.

The example shown above proves the point that *every* player has something to do on nearly every defensive play, especially with runners on base. You must get this fact through to your players so they will be on their toes, physically and mentally, in anticipation of the next play. Too often you will see an inexperienced player start to think, "Where should I throw the ball?" or "Where should I go?" *after* the ball has been hit, when you should have taught him to think about what he should do *before* the ball is hit. If you get the point across to him that he has to do *something*—either cover the ball or cover a base—then he will start anticipating his move.

Only drilling will make this happen automatically, and players must be drilled mentally as well as physically. Take advantage of the practice rainouts and use the time for skull sessions. Describe game situations and assign positions to your players on paper (realistically, positions they will probably play). Then ask each to tell where he should anticipate going on each play that could happen in that situation. (Examples of such questions are in the quiz at the end of this chapter.)

*3. Always throw to one base ahead of the runner.* An inexperienced right fielder, after fielding a single, will throw the ball to first base, and a savvy base runner, having made the turn, will go to second. A well-taught outfielder will always throw to one base ahead of the base that the lead runner will obviously reach. To put it another way, tell your outfielders, in anticipation that the batter will get a single to his field, to count two bases ahead of the base the lead runner is on; that is the base he should be ready to throw to. Thus, on a single with no one on base, he will throw to second (two bases ahead of home); with a man on first, he will throw to third on a single (two bases ahead of the base occupied by the lead runner); on a single with a runner on second, the outfielder will throw home; and so forth.

*4. With a runner on base, get the lead runner.* The most obvious and most commonly seen example is making the force play at second. This play is easier to make in Little League than in advanced leagues since the base runner cannot lead off. By the same token, double plays are less frequent in Little League because the hitter has only 60 feet to run to first base during the time that the force play is being made. For that reason, I drill the force play in every possible situation, over and over, and minimize the time spent drilling the double play. If you question this reasoning, use runners in practice and see how few double plays your boys can make; obviously, even fewer in a game situation.

The number of passed balls and wild pitches in Little League, giving the runner on first a free ride to second, also limits the number of opportunities for a double play. Yet you will see many coaches devote so much time to drilling their infield in "getting two" that you would think it was a frequent play. By drilling your boys too much in the double play, when the odds in Little League are against their making it, you risk forcing bad throws that could result in two men on base instead of two outs. Better to concentrate on the basic play of getting the lead runner.

Selecting the boys that will play each position is the key to setting up your best defense. "Strong up the middle" is the best rule to follow: catcher, pitcher, shortstop, second base, and center field are the positions for your best players. With your best players giving you a strong defense up the middle, and with much attention paid to drilling the basics, your Little League team should be good defensively. There are also some fine points in defensive strategy that you as coach, rather than your players, can contribute, and they will be covered in Chapter 11.

The following quiz will sharpen your players' defensive play.

## LITTLE LEAGUE BASEBALL QUIZ: DEFENSIVE PLAY

*Note:* Use the following abbreviations in answering some questions:

| | | |
|---|---|---|
| 1B: first baseman | LF: left fielder | C: catcher |
| 2B: second baseman | CF: center fielder | P: pitcher |
| 3B: third baseman | RF: right fielder | H: home plate |
| SS: shortstop | | |

Circle *T* or *F* for the true-and-false questions. Write the correct answers in the blanks for the other questions.

1. In throwing a ball, a right-
   hander should step toward the
   target with his left foot.　　　　　　T　　　　　　F

2. The outfielder should always
   throw to the base ahead of the
   lead runner.　　　　　　　　　　　T　　　　　　F

3. When a batter singles with a
   runner on first, the outfielder
   should throw to second base.　　　T　　　　　　F

4. When a batter singles with a
   runner on second, the
   outfielder should throw the ball
   home.　　　　　　　　　　　　　T　　　　　　F

5. The bull's-eye in throwing to
   another fielder is between his
   waist and his shoulder.　　　　　T　　　　　　F

6. On a ball hit to the outfield,
   who backs up . . . the left
   fielder?　　　　　　　　　　　_____

7. . . . the right fielder?　　　　　　_____

8. . . . the center fielder when he
   catches a ball in left center
   field?　　　　　　　　　　　　_____

9. . . . the center fielder when he
   catches a ball in right center
   field?　　　　　　　　　　　　_____

10. On ground balls hit to the
    outfield between first and
    second, who is the relay man?　_____

11. On ground balls hit to the
    outfield between second and
    third, who is the relay man?　　_____

12. When catching a ball, you should turn your head so you don't take a chance of getting hit in the face.　　　　T　　　　F

13. An infielder should look a ball into his glove to remind himself to keep his eyes on the ball.　　　　T　　　　F

14. It isn't necessary to use two hands in catching a fly ball.　　　　T　　　　F

15. When no one is out, no one is on base, and the batter singles to right field, . . . who fields the ball?　　　_____

16. . . . what base does he throw to?　　　_____

17. . . . who takes the throw at that base?　　　_____

18. When no one is out, no one is on base, and the batter singles to left field, . . . who fields the ball?　　　_____

19. . . . what base does he throw to?　　　_____

20. . . . who takes the throw?　　　_____

21. When no one is out, a runner is on first, and the batter doubles to right field, . . . who fields the ball?　　　_____

22. . . . who fields the relay?　　　_____

23. . . . what base does he throw to?　　　_____

24. . . . who covers that base?　　　_____

25. . . . who backs him up?                    _____

26. When no one is out, runners
    are on first and second, and
    the batter singles to right
    center field, . . . who fields the
    ball?                                       _____

27. . . . who backs him up?                    _____

28. . . . what base does he throw
    to?                                         _____

29. . . . who covers that base?                _____

30. . . . who backs him up?                    _____

31. With a runner on third base
    and fewer than two outs, the
    batter hits a short fly ball that
    you can catch . . . you should
    assume the runner will try to
    score after the catch.            T                    F

32. . . . you should throw the ball
    to what base?                               _____

33. . . . who should cover that
    base?                                       _____

34. . . . who should back him up?              _____

35. When a runner is on second,
    there are fewer than two outs,
    and a fly ball is hit to center
    field, . . . you should assume
    the runner will try to go to
    third after the catch.            T                    F

36. . . . you should throw the ball
    to what base?                               _____

37. . . . who should cover that
    base?                                       _____

38. . . . who should back him up?              _____

39. When a right-handed batter is up and the runner on first attempts to steal, who should take the throw from the catcher? _____

40. When a left-handed batter is up and the runner on first attempts to steal, who should take the throw from the catcher? _____

41. Who backs up the play when the second baseman takes the throw from the catcher on an attempted steal? _____

42. With a runner trapped between first and second, . . . who should back up the first baseman? _____

43. . . . who should back up the second baseman? _____

44. With a runner trapped between second and third, . . . who should back up the second baseman? _____

45. . . . Who should back up the third baseman? _____

46. With a runner trapped between third and home, . . . who should back up the third baseman? _____

47. . . . who should back up the catcher? _____

48. In chasing down a trapped runner, always chase him back to the base he left.          T                    F

49. In a bunt down the first baseline that the first baseman must field, who covers first base to take the throw? _____

50. In a bunt down the third baseline that the third baseman must field, who covers third base? _____

51. This was an easy quiz.　　　　T　　　　　F

_____        _____  _____
　　　　PRINT NAME　　　　　　DATE　　SCORE

**ANSWER KEY**

| | | | | |
|---|---|---|---|---|
| 1. T | 12. F | 23. H | 34. P | 45. P |
| 2. T | 13. T | 24. C | 35. T | 46. SS |
| 3. F | 14. F | 25. P | 36. 3B | 47. P |
| 4. T | 15. RF | 26. RF | 37. 3B | 48. T |
| 5. T | 16. 2B | 27. CF | 38. P | 49. 2B |
| 6. CF | 17. 2B | 28. H | 39. 2B | 50. SS |
| 7. CF | 18. LF | 29. C | 40. SS | 51. T |
| 8. LF | 19. 2B | 30. P | 41. SS | |
| 9. RF | 20. SS | 31. T | 42. P | |
| 10. 2B | 21. RF | 32. H | 43. SS | |
| 11. SS | 22. 2B | 33. C | 44. SS | |

# 7
# DRILLING
# THE BASICS:
## PITCHING

Ask any Little League manager how important pitching is to the success of his team, and you will get answers in the range of 60–80 percent. Ironically, however, the amount of practice time devoted to pitching is more like 10 percent. The primary reason for this is that pitching practice, unless it is in intrasquad game practice, interferes with team fielding and hitting practice (which require the use of the mound and the plate). Chapter 8 outlines a practice drill that allows your pitchers and catchers to practice, using the mound and plate, while at the same time your infielders are taking ground ball practice and your outfielders are shagging (practicing catching) flies. But in addition to integrating pitching practice into team practice, extra practice outside of team practice will be necessary if you are to develop strong pitchers. If you believe that good pitching is 60–80 percent of a successful team, isn't the added practice justified?

## CHOOSING AND SCHEDULING PITCHERS

Nearly every Little Leaguer would like to pitch; it's the glamor position from which stars are made. When All Star team balloting is done (by the players and coaches in our league), invariably the pitchers are the boys who get the most votes, and more than one

All Star manager has bemoaned the fact that he has a squad of 14 pitchers and not one experienced catcher! The boy who gets his first taste of Little League pitching soon discovers that it is not as glamorous as he thought. Pitching is hard work, fraught with tension, and to be a good Little League pitcher a boy must be physically strong and emotionally cool.

Too often we see in Little League what I call the "manager's son/pitcher syndrome": the manager or coach who is determined to make his son a pitcher when often the boy does not have the physical strength and emotional coolness and may not even want to pitch. The father-coach/son-player relationship then becomes particularly strained, because the son tries so hard—sometimes too hard—to live up to his dad's expectations. If your son wants to pitch, has the qualifications, and is a better prospect than his teammates, then by all means give him the opportunity. But above all, resist the temptation to try to make him a pitcher if he doesn't have the qualifications, and particularly if he doesn't have the desire. There are still eight other positions on the team for him to play.

Since the rules allow only two 12-year-old pitchers to be used in a week, you are well-advised to narrow down your pitching prospects to six boys: two 12-year-olds, two 11-year-olds, and two 10-year-olds. Normally your number one and two pitchers will be your 12-year-olds since they will be the physically stronger, more experienced boys. Invariably your number one pitcher will be the best athlete on the team—not only the best pitcher but probably the best hitter, best fielder, best everything. Since he has the strongest arm, he will often be your shortstop when he isn't pitching—the second position on the team requiring the best of everything. Frequently, you will find a Little League team using its number one or two pitcher in the catching position when he isn't pitching. I try to avoid that, if possible, since catchers are more prone to injuries than any other position, and a jammed finger on his pitching hand is something one of your ace pitchers doesn't need. An ideal rotation would be for your number one and two pitchers to rotate between pitching and playing shortstop. In that way they will be the only two regulars who must play two positions.

Like the football coach who has to give his backup quarterback some experience this year to prepare him to be number one next year, you must do the same for your backup pitchers.

Our league schedule calls for two games a week, and theoretically we could use just two good pitchers in the entire season. If your schedule calls for more than two games a week, you obviously cannot get by with only two pitchers, but even with a two-game-a-week schedule, a rainout, forcing a third game in the next week, will create problems for you if you haven't concentrated on training more than two pitchers. And an extra-inning game will court disaster. Several years ago, in a close game that had a direct bearing on the league championship, the game was tied as we went to bat in the bottom of the sixth; our number one pitcher had pitched all six innings, and our number two pitcher had used up his eligibility in the earlier game that week. Our number three pitcher, Jimmy, an 11-year-old, was second to bat in the bottom of the sixth, so he couldn't even start warming up until he came back to the dugout. As he headed for the on-deck circle, he confirmed his worst fears when he asked, "Am I going to have to pitch if we don't score the winning run this inning?" I answered, "Yes, so let's get a run!" The first batter got a walk and went to second on a passed ball. Jimmy looked over at me and nodded, then promptly jumped on the first pitch for a clean single that scored the second run. I am convinced that the added incentive—in this case not wanting to pitch—helped him get that game-winning hit. He liked to pitch but, being inexperienced, didn't especially welcome gaining his experience in that pressure-filled situation.

Physical strength, which is usually related to size, is the primary attribute you should look for in a prospective pitcher. Since the fastball is the predominant pitch in Little League, it stands to reason that bigger, stronger boys will be able to throw more "smoke." As always, there are exceptions, such as a small, wiry boy who, despite his size, has good arm strength.

I remember two brothers at Little League baseball camp several summers ago; one had picked up the nickname "A.C.," and the other, of course, answered to "D.C." They were small and wiry and didn't look like your typical Little League pitchers, but the first time I umpired behind the plate when A.C. was pitching I realized that looks were deceiving. He had a blazing fastball, an excellent curveball, and a deceptive change-up; in addition, he had the most important skill of all for Little League pitchers—control. After the game I asked A.C. to show me his grip for his curveball, and he asked, "Which one?" He was cocky, he was cool, and after I got to know him better, I realized that he was truly dedicated, which made up for his lack of physical size. Baseball and pitching were his life! He was at baseball camp on a scholarship, coming from an inner-city environment where the best opportunity to gain recognition is through athletics. It is the same environment that has spawned so many basketball superstars, when a basketball rim and a ball and hours of practice paid off. I think A.C. realized he was too short for basketball, so he spent his hours of practice pitching baseballs to his brother 12 months a year!

Suburban and country kids have a choice of so many activities that it is rare to find a boy *that* dedicated to baseball coming from one of those environments. But from whatever environment, there must be an above-average degree of dedication to the extra practice required, in addition to physical strength and emotional coolness, if a boy is to become a good Little League pitcher. Control doesn't come easily, but it does come with dedication to practice *every day,* not just when the rest of the team practices. That, of course, requires someone for the pitcher to pitch to: his dad, brother, or coach (if *he* is that dedicated).

Our team was blessed with three brothers, two years apart in age, with a dad who was a former semipro catcher. You can be sure that pitching was practiced every day in their backyard, and the results showed. The youngest brother became the best pitcher, because he learned so much from his older brothers as they advanced into Senior League, High School, Big League, and college baseball.

Physical strength, a fastball, and good control are the necessary tools of a good Little League pitcher, and I have seen many pitchers who were very successful without a curve or a change-up. Some Little League pitchers claim a repertoire of pitches that they really don't have, like A.C., who asked me which of his curveballs I wanted to see. Frequently a good fastball will "tail off" as it crosses the plate, and the batter and catcher will both swear they saw a curve. When I refer to a fastball "tailing," I mean the visual impression that the pitch drops or curves from the straight line that a fastball normally takes. Technically, every fastball has some arc to it, caused by gravity, but the way the ball is gripped and/or the way it spins out of the pitcher's hand will affect the normal arc and make the pitch drop or curve just before it reaches home plate. Experimentation, lots of practice, and good communication between pitcher and catcher will help a pitcher develop variations of his fastball. Some coaches claim that a fastball thrown with the fingers across the seams, instead of parallel to them, will make the fastball "tail" and appear to curve. When that happens your catcher should reinforce the myth by saying loud and clear, "Nice curveball, Charlie." Psychologically, it is good for the other team to think your pitcher has more pitches than he actually does.

## THE FASTBALL

Since the underlying theme of this book is "stick to the basics," the basics of Little League pitching are a fastball and control. Statistically, the odds are about 60/40 that every walk your pitcher gives up will result in a run; so a pitcher who yields no walks in a six-inning game will surely win. If his control is that good, then he should be able to place his pitches as well. And if he keeps his fastball low on the first four or five batters in the opposing lineup, the worst that will happen is that they will hit the ball on the ground and end up with infield outs, assuming your infield is sound. Your pitcher can then challenge the bottom four or five batters in the lineup with his fastball anywhere in the strike zone.

Most inexperienced Little League pitchers fail to gain the full potential of their fastball by pitching with their wrists and arms instead of with their whole body. A training technique that will force a pitcher to use his shoulder and back is to hold his right foot (for a right-handed pitcher) as he pitches. Without being able to move that foot, he is forced to bend his shoulder and back to gain any velocity in his pitches. He immediately becomes aware of how much stronger velocity and better control he can gain when he pitches with his body.

## THE CHANGE-UP

If your pitcher can add a change-up to his fastball, he will have an even greater advantage over the good hitters. A change-up on an 0 and 2 or 1 and 2 count will usually fool them. A change-up is easy for a pitcher to learn, but the ability to throw it consistently within the strike zone is again a question of dedication. How much extra time is he willing to devote to throwing it over and over again until he can control it? The grip is the same as with a fastball: index and middle finger on top; thumb underneath; except that the ball is palmed instead of held away from the hand, as with a fastball or

Changing the grip on the fastball will make the ball behave differently.

curve. Some pitchers feel it is easier to control with three fingers on top. The delivery is also similar to the fastball, except that just at the time of release the hand should be pulled down quickly to give the ball the float that is so destructive to a tense batter's timing. A pitcher should throw a change-up only to a good hitter, never to a poor hitter, for whom a fastball is always the best pitch.

As mentioned earlier in the chapter on rules, you should teach your pitchers to pitch from the set position when they are having control problems since they will gain in control, although they will

When you hold a pitcher's rubber foot in practice, it forces him to use his shoulder and back to gain maximum ball speed.

lose some speed by pitching from this position. However, when pitching to the lower end of the batting order, a pitcher can afford to sacrifice speed for control. The worst thing he can do is give up a walk to a weak hitter.

## EMOTIONAL COOLNESS

In addition to physical strength, the other major quality of a good pitcher is emotional coolness. So much depends on the pitcher, particularly in Little League, that he must be a boy who can stand the pressure. He is the team leader, and if he loses his cool, it will have an effect on the morale of the whole team. We have stressed the importance of concentration, and in no position is it more important than for the pitcher. As his coach, you need to remind him to be mentally deaf to the jibes of the fans or the other team and mentally oblivious to the umpire's calls. Persuade him that, for every call that goes against him, there will be one that goes for him. Umpires aren't infallible, but they do have a tendency to average their bad calls. Regular umpires will tend to be consistent—either bad or good—and knowing your umpires is a strategy that will be covered in Chapter 11.

To help your pitcher gain confidence and keep his cool, his teammates have to be vocally supportive. A struggling pitcher doesn't need a teammate shouting, "Come on Charlie, get it over the plate." He needs to hear "Come on Charlie, you can do it." I recommend a routine after a strikeout (with no one on base) that is a real confidence builder for the pitcher and has the opposite effect on the on-deck batter. It is mentioned in Chapter 11.

Practicing the basics in pitching to gain control and spending the extra hours perfecting a change-up and/or a curve require a degree of dedication that only an A.C. with a special kind of motivation could be expected to apply without the constant practice becoming a tiresome bore. If it isn't fun, the average Little League pitcher soon loses interest. Chapter 8 includes some tips on how to make practicing the basics of pitching fun, even when the boys are doing the extra practicing on their own.

# 8

# PRACTICE:
## MAKE IT SIMPLE, KEEP IT FUN

The mission of a Little League Manager is to teach, but he has one disadvantage in comparison to a schoolteacher. If his student isn't having any fun, he may choose something else to learn that *is* fun. Throughout this book I have emphasized the importance of sticking to the basics, but practice can be real drudgery if the drills are monotonous and/or don't involve all of the players. So you are well advised to keep your practice sessions simple but make them fun. By finding ways to make simple drills competitive, or similar to game situations, you will automatically make them fun. And, by all means, combine drills in such a way that all boys are involved and busy.

To keep all boys active in practice sessions at the same time, you will need coaching help. I feel that a manager and at least two coaches are necessary to provide an adequate coaching staff. Even with just three, there will be occasions when one or more of the coaches will be unable to help at a practice session because of work or personal schedule conflicts. I have never had a problem finding at least two other dedicated dads, among a squad of 14 or 15 boys, who were more than willing to get involved. Many dads would love to help, are too bashful to volunteer, but are grateful to be asked.

But, as is the case with their sons, they need to be kept busy, or they will get bored, too. Find out what each feels he can contribute most, based on his background, but, as mentioned earlier, don't take a chance of embarrassing a dad in front of the boys by asking him to do something unless you are sure he can. Consult with your coaches frequently; ask their advice; share your objectives with them. Some of them may be pretty rusty on Little League rules, so provide them with rule books and any other "homework" that can help them be more effective.

One of the first frustrations you will face as a new coach or manager is the lack of practice time. If your league is like most, the number of teams wanting to practice will far exceed the number of practice fields available. Add to that early spring cold and rainy weather, and you will soon realize that the basics are all that practice time can practically permit. You will also quickly realize that making the most efficient use of the practice time available is mandatory.

## WARM-UP DRILLS

Practice should start as soon as the first boy arrives. Conditioning exercises should take first priority, but rather than waste valuable practice time by waiting for all boys to arrive for group calisthenics, I recommend having each boy do individual stretching exercises as he arrives. Here's a simple individual drill:

1. Give a boy a bat and have him hold it at arm's length like a wand, one hand on each end.
2. Then have him bend at the waist, keep legs straight, and stretch his legs as he attempts to touch the ground with the bat.
3. Then have him rise while holding the bat away from the body until he is stretching it over his head.
4. Then have him stretch the torso by bringing the outstretched hands first to one side and then to the other.
5. Finally, he should bring the bat down behind his back, even with his butt.

This simple exercise, done 10 times, will stretch leg, arm, chest, and back muscles. Follow this with wind sprints: run from home to first and walk back, three times. Then, as boys finish their individual warm-up drills, have them pair off and start throwing the ball, first at 20 feet and gradually increasing to 60 feet, which is the distance between bases.

This is the first drill you can make into a competitive game. When the boys reach the 60-foot distance, they can play "Five and Ten," a game designed to sharpen their throwing accuracy. Hitting the other player's glove at chest level is worth 5 points; at head level it is worth 10 points; anyplace else, no points. The first player to reach 50 points wins.

## AROUND THE HORN DRILL

In the first few practice sessions, you will want to evaluate what talent you have and what weaknesses you need to concentrate on. Boys hate to be relegated to one position too early without being given a chance at all positions. So they enjoy a drill we call "Around the Horn," because it gives every player a chance to play every fielding position. We do it with two coaches hitting balls simultaneously, one positioned between home and first and the other between home and third. Each has a boy catching the throw-ins for him. The coach between home and first hits ground balls to the shortstop and third baseman and fly balls to the left fielder and a left center fielder. The coach between home and third hits ground balls to the first and second basemen and fly balls to the right fielder and a right center fielder. The infielders, after fielding a ground ball, aim for accuracy in throwing to the "catcher"; the outfielders, after catching or fielding a ball, aim for accuracy in throwing to the relay man, who pivots and aims for accuracy in throwing to the catcher. The drill keeps 10 boys active at the same time. After each boy has had three chances at a position, you rotate everyone clockwise, with the right fielder going to the first base catching position and the first baseman going to the third base catching spot. The third base catcher rotates to left field, and the first base catcher moves to third base; so, the first time "around the horn," a boy will play all outfield positions and the second time all infield positions.

If you have more than 10 boys and more than two coaches, you can have your pitchers and catchers warming up at the same time, because the pitcher's mound and home plate are not used in this drill. Whenever a pitcher is practicing, I recommend that you have

### FIGURE 1. "AROUND THE HORN" PRACTICE ROUTINE (USING AS MANY AS 2 COACHES AND 15 PLAYERS)

KEY: Ⓒ Coach
C  Catcher
B  Batter
P  Pitcher
F  Outfielder
Ground Ball ▬▬▬▬▬▬▬
Fly Ball ••••••••••••••••••

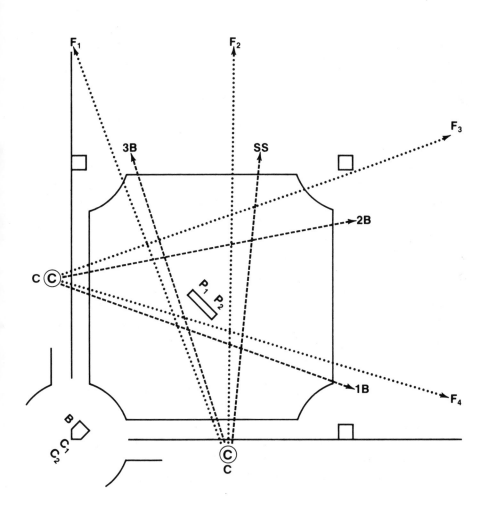

a batter at home plate—with a bat and a helmet on, of course—doing everything except hitting the ball. It is amazing how many pitchers, after warming up with their catcher, can't find the plate when a batter steps into the batting box. The whole perspective of the plate changes. That's why I feel it is important for a pitcher to warm up with a batter in the box, so his practice is as gamelike as possible.

In this combination drill, the throw-ins from the fielders will be on a straight line to the third base or first base "catchers," so there should be no balls thrown across the pitcher's mound to interfere with your pitcher's practice. If you have 2 pitchers, 2 catchers, and a batter taking part in this pitcher/catcher drill, combined with the 10 boys involved in the fielders' drill, you will have 15 boys and 3 coaches involved in active practice simultaneously and on one field! It will be a fun drill the boys will enjoy, at the same time giving the coaches a chance to view every boy at every position.

## OUTFIELD/INFIELD DRILL

I go from that drill to what we call the "Outfield/Infield Drill." You should start with your 6 players, who make up your first team infield for the infield part of the drill, plus 3 runners. Two teams of 3 players each will participate in the outfield drill. That allows you to have a total of 15 boys actively practicing at the same time on one field. Rotating the boys from the outfield to the infield to runners will again give them a chance at various positions, but as your defensive team starts to jell, you will want to concentrate more practice time with the boys in the positions they will probably play.

The outfield drill can be made into a competitive game between teams of three. Each team will have an outfielder, a relay man, and a catcher. Two points are scored for catching a fly ball, one point when the outfielder hits the relay man with a throw between chest and head, and one point when the relay man pivots and throws a strike to the catcher. After an outfielder has a chance to catch three fly balls, the members of his team rotate positions, and after each boy has played all three positions, you total each team's score.

In the infield drill, a coach calls plays—e.g., "No outs, nobody on"—and hits grounders with runners simulating game conditions. The time should be spent drilling the most common plays, e.g., the ground out to first and the force out to each of the bases. Double

## FIGURE 2. OUTFIELD/INFIELD PRACTICE ROUTINE
## (USING AS MANY AS 3 COACHES AND 15 PLAYERS)

KEY: Ⓒ Coach
    **R** Runner

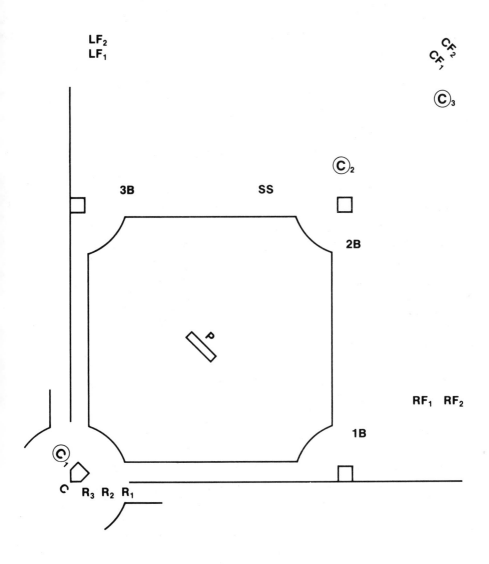

plays are so rare in Little League that they should be given minimal practice time, in my opinion. As a matter of fact, there is a danger in overdrilling the double play to the point that the pivot man will feel he *has* to make the play at first and will rush the play, with resulting fielding and/or throwing errors. I would rather spend the time drilling to get the lead runner on force plays to second, third, and home.

## HITTING DRILLS

The most difficult practice drill of all is hitting practice because it is so difficult to keep many boys active at the same time if you have only one field.

A surprising number of Little League teams have only one practice drill for hitting: pitching to the batters, one at a time. Yet it is the least efficient hitting drill possible in terms of number of swings and hits a batter can take per minute of practice time. Unless you have a pitching machine that always pitches in the strike zone, the basics of hitting can't be practiced enough to become automatic if this is the only opportunity each of your boys has to practice hitting. With a 15-player roster, if you did nothing else in a one-and-one-half-hour practice session but practiced batting, you would provide only six minutes of batting practice time per player. But you rarely will devote *full* practice time to hitting; more realistically, half of the practice would be batting practice, which reduces the time allocated to each player to three minutes. Allowing for pitches not in the strike zone, missed strikes, called strikes, fouled strikes, and throwing time between pitcher and catcher, *an individual player is lucky to get much more than a minute of actual batting time* (time spent on the practical drill of hitting the ball with the bat). If you don't believe me, time and count in your next batting practice. Is it any wonder that so few boys hit so few balls in so few games?

The most inefficient aspect of the all-too-typical hitting drill of pitching to one batter at a time is the obvious fact that only one batter can hit at a time! The team drill *is* important, not just as a hitting drill, but as a pitching, hitting, running, and fielding drill as well. But to prepare your players properly for the coordination of all of those skills, each must be drilled separately before they are brought together.

There are six hitting drills that I have found helpful, varying from one drill one boy can do alone to a team drill:

1. One-player drill
2. Two-player (or player-coach) drill
3. Pepper drill (three or four players)
4. Batting tee drill (any number of players)
5. Pitching/hitting drill (any number of players)
6. Team drill (pitching/hitting/running/fielding/base coaching)

## Individual Drill

It struck me as being significant that a rookie can't hit a ball out of his hand (throw the ball up and hit it). I think it is significant because the three basics of hitting are involved in this exercise: concentration, arms back, and stride/swing. Even though the ball is thrown in a vertical plane, the batter has to be able to concentrate on it to judge his timing; getting the arms back is a necessary movement, because his hand is in front of the body when he throws the ball up; and then the stride/swing is a natural movement as he hits the ball.

This is a drill that will allow as many boys to practice at the same time as there are available balls and bats. I line up the boys facing a fence so they are hitting into the fence and don't have far to go to retrieve the ball. If you try the drill yourself and keep repeating it, you will feel a batting rhythm set in (concentration, arms back, stride/swing) that is exactly what you want the young hitters to develop. The reason the young hitters initially have trouble with this drill is that they haven't developed the eye, arm, and leg coordination—in short, the rhythm—necessary to become a hitter.

The rookies will be frustrated at first by their awkward attempts to hit the ball out of their hand. Better to have them awkward at that stage than in games when the season starts. Gradually, with your help and encouragement, they will pick up the rhythm and hit the ball consistently. To mark their progress, have them keep track of how many hits they make for each ten attempts and watch their percentages increase each day—not to mention their self-confidence.

A player should be able to take 16 swings per minute, so if you devote six minutes of practice time to *this* drill, each batter will swing the bat *nearly 100 times!* Multiply that by the number of batters you have participating in this drill simultaneously (10 would equal 1,000!), and you can see how much more efficient this kind of drill is than a six-minute drill of the typical kind with one boy at bat and someone pitching to him.

This drill should include bunting as well as hitting practice. The batter can easily square around into the bunting position and assume the proper hand positions on the bat as he throws the ball in the air. He will start to observe how bat position will vary the direction of the batted ball and how coming down on the ball will keep it on the ground instead of popping it up. These observations will translate themselves into automatic techniques as the bunting drills continue in each practice. When he starts to practice hitting against pitching, he will surprise you (and himself) at how good a bunter he can be. You may have questioned my earlier claim that it is easier for a Little Leaguer to bunt than to hit, but if you give it equal time in your early drills, I think you will find this to be true.

## Two-Player Drill

This is a modification of the previous drill and can be coordinated with it. The batter is still facing and hitting into a fence (or backstop). The other player or coach kneels beside him to the right of the "plate" and toward the fence, as you face the fence (for a right-handed batter). Instead of having the batter throw the ball up in a vertical plane, have the other player or coach throw it in from the side. This gives the batter the opportunity to assume a normal batting stance as he awaits the ball. The coach can observe the things the batter does when he swings and can correct them (if necessary) before bad habits set in. This is where the 28 different things involved in hitting—e.g., arms away from the body, level swing, chin on the shoulder—can be observed by the coach. The coach can add them systematically to the drill once the boy has combined the three basics into an automatic rhythm. If he adds them one at a time, and the batter is practicing them in his swing 100 times per practice session, each improvement will become an integral and automatic part of his rhythm.

Two-player batting drill: player at right throws in balls, and batter hits them into backstop.

## Pepper Drill

This is a combination hitting and fielding drill designed to develop rhythm patterns in both skills. It involves one batter facing three fielders in a semicircle, with the middle fielder about 30 feet away and the other two ringed closer. A fielder will start the drill by lobbing the ball (overhand) to the batter, who meets it hard enough to one-hop it to a fielder, who in one continuous motion scoops up the ball and throws the next pitch. Both the pitching and the hitting are done at about half-speed, with the objective being to keep the ball in play quickly and continuously. The hitter should mix hitting and bunting. When he bunts and a fielder has to move in to field the ball, he pivots and tosses the ball back to one of the other fielders in order to keep the ball in constant play.

Once they get the hang of it, your boys will enjoy this drill and will try to see how long (and how fast) they can keep the ball in constant play without interruption.

If you have ever seen a professional baseball team engage in this drill, you can almost feel the rhythm of the batter as he hits every pitch and the fielders handle the ball in a smooth, sure motion. That is the kind of dual rhythm that should be the goal of a pepper drill. The drill can be staged anywhere, but is best held on the infield or another smooth-surfaced field so the batted ball will take a true bounce.

Once your team is adept at this drill, you can have three teams of 5 players using the infield simultaneously. One batter stands in front of the pitcher's mound, facing the backstop, and the fielders

Pepper drill: one batter and three infielders try to keep ball in play.

are ringed around home plate. The second batter stands to the side of the pitcher's mound, facing the baseline between first and second bases; the third batter stands to the side of the pitcher's mound, facing the baseline between second and third bases. Three players (and/or coaches) should stand on the pitcher's mound, one backing up each batter to keep balls from going through and interfering with one of the other groups. If you have 15 boys on your roster, you can divide them into three groups, each group with a batter, 3 fielders, and a retriever. Each batter hits 10 and bunts 10, and then the group rotates positions. When all three groups have completed their respective cycles, *300 balls will have been hit and fielded!* That is drilling the basics to develop rhythm!

Dive drill: coach throws balls to left or right of infielders to get them used to diving for infield balls.

## Batting Tee Drill

If you have no tee, ask your local highway department garage to donate one of its large rubber marker cones. Insert a radiator hose in the top, and you have a tee! Batting off the tee is a good introduction to hitting since it gives the coach a chance to check these batting basics:

- size of bat
- bat grip
- stance
- arms back
- stride/swing

The batting coach should check these basics with each succeeding boy as he comes to the plate, letting him take a few practice swings to make corrections.

There are two drills that can be done with the batting tee. One is a hitting/fielding drill; the other is a hitting/fielding/base running drill.

## *Hitting/Fielding Drill*

In the hitting/fielding drill, each hitter hits three and bunts three, and the fielders field the batted ball (as though the hitter were up with no outs and no one on base). To make the hitting and timing as realistic as possible, the fielding pitcher goes through his motion and pretends to pitch the ball (as is done in the Minor League T-Ball program). This gives the hitter the opportunity to practice the hitting rhythm of concentration, arms back, and stride/swing and the bunting rhythm as well.

The batter can feel the difference between hitting the ball when the rhythm is well coordinated and hitting it when it isn't. For example, if you tell a boy to hit the ball off the tee without striding, he quickly understands how important the stride is in bringing his full power into the ball. Similarly, if you tell him to swing up or chop down on the ball, he will feel the positive difference when he uses a level swing. In bunting, he will get the feel of accurately controlling the direction and flight of the bunt through the positioning of his bat.

### *Hitting/Fielding/Base Running/Base Coaching Drill*

After every player has had a turn at hitting three and bunting three off the tee, in rotation, you can then go to the second drill involving the tee. This is the hitting/fielding/base running/base coaching drill. After putting a defensive team in the field, assign the remaining players as batter/runners and base coaches. Stealing is the only game situation that can't be allowed, but otherwise, hitting, base running, and fielding strategy apply, depending on the number of outs. Before you give the signal to the pitcher to go into his mock windup, the defensive coach should make sure the infielders have signaled the number of outs and any other instructions to each other (e.g., "Get the lead man at second," "The play's to first," etc.). The offensive coach should, at the same time, be checking to see that the base coaches have done their jobs if there are runners on base, such as reminding the runners of the number of outs, telling them that there are other runners on base, instructing them to "run on anything" if there are two outs, and so on.

As the pitcher follows through with his mock pitch and goes into his fielding position, the batter hits the ball off the tee, and the ball is in play in a simulated game situation. In the course of the batting tee drill, you will encounter most of the usual base running and defensive fielding situations that will occur later in games.

You should substitute the hitters and base coaches into the fielding positions they will probably play, eventually rotating your players so they all have a chance to bat off the tee.

## Pitching/Hitting Drill

It should be noted that four batting drills have been recommended prior to using this drill that involve actual pitching from the pitcher's mound to the plate. Ideally, a pitching machine could be utilized, but since most Little League teams don't have access to one, a coach or good control pitcher should be used to ensure that a high percentage of pitches go into the strike zone. But the pitcher should throw at Little League speed. The drill requires a pitcher, catcher, and three or more retrievers. Since it is a hitting drill only, the job of the retrievers is to field the ball and quickly get it back to the pitcher so the hitting can be continuous. To keep the drill moving quickly, the pitcher can handle three balls at a time (two in his glove and one in his pitching hand). If he pitches them one after the other, without waiting for the catcher to return the ball after every pitch, he can pitch more and the hitter can hit more per minute of practice time. While one fielder is retrieving the batted ball, the pitcher can be delivering the next one. When the pitcher has no more balls to pitch, the catcher and/or fielders can return them all to him at the same time.

As mentioned earlier, bunting should be practiced initially to get the hitter used to concentrating on the pitched ball. The batter will want to hit away, but make him earn that by showing that he can bunt first. In early practice sessions, especially, I recommend that at least half of the batting practice be devoted to bunting, not just to perfect the bunting skill, but to achieve the two goals that bunting practice will help achieve: (1) improving concentration and (2) overcoming the fear of being hit.

In order to give all boys an equal opportunity at batting practice, I recommend you divide the planned practice time at bat by time intervals, rather than by number of hits, which is what most coaches make the mistake of doing. You can divide the amount of time for batting practice by the number of players and then make sure that each boy gets an equal time at bat. Otherwise, you will invariably run out of time, and the last few boys will not get their fair turns at bat. Since this batting drill involves only five or six players (pitcher or pitching coach, catcher, batter, and three fielders), it should be used in conjunction with other drills so that all boys are active in practice at the same time. Pitchers and catchers could be practicing at the same time at another location, and/or a coach could be hitting fly balls in the outfield-to-relay-man-to-catcher drill, described earlier in this chapter, a drill that can keep six boys actively practicing other skills at the same time that their teammates are going through the batting drill. Then the groups change position after each player in the hitting drill has batted.

## Team Drill

This is a fun drill that your boys will enjoy because it comes closest to simulating actual game conditions. Since you will be practicing four skills—hitting, pitching, running, and defense—it would be ideal if you could have four coaches, each watching and coaching one of the four skills. With only two coaches, one can coach the hitting and base running, the other the pitching and defense.

The pitching coach can stand on the mound and double as umpire, calling balls and strikes to add game realism to the drill. It is advisable to have two pitchers working, alternating with each three outs. To use this primarily as a batting drill—but still simulate game conditions—I suggest that you have each batter take three turns at bat in succession at two different times. With a 15-player roster, you will have 9 defensive players, an extra pitcher, a batter, 2 runners, and 2 base coaches. As the batter hits or walks, a runner will run for him.

This drill can be used for an intersquad game by dividing your 15-player squad into two 6-man teams, plus a rotating outfield. By rotating players who have batted to the outfield at the end of each half-inning, you will give all boys an equal opportunity to bat and play defense. Although there is a natural temptation to want to schedule practice games with other teams early in the practice season, unless it represents an extra practice session, you will be sacrificing half of your team's valuable practice time when you do. There will be plenty of opportunity for game competition when the season starts, but understanding the basics of hitting and drilling them until they become automatic should be the preseason priorities.

## SITUATION DRILLS

In addition to basic fielding, hitting, and base running drills, there are additional situation drills that should be inserted into your practice sessions from time to time.

### Stealing Practice

Stealing practice, combined with defending against the steal, is one of these. A good time to stage this drill is when the ground is soft, for obvious reasons. Since this drill is particularly demanding of your catcher, be prepared to substitute at that position. To keep the practice moving, borrow a second set of catcher's gear from another team so your substitute catcher can step right into the drill and not delay it by having to wait for your catchers to exchange equipment.

To practice steals at second base, you will need a batter, pitcher, catcher, first baseman, second baseman, shortstop, center fielder, and substitute catcher. The rest of your players can line up at first base and take turns stealing. One adult coach can work with the runners, another with the defense. Then practice steals of third and finally steals of home. As mentioned in the chapter on base running, stealing home could make the difference between winning and losing a ball game. The potential opportunity of being safe is much better in Little League than in higher-level play for these reasons.

1. There are only 60 feet to travel.
2. There are more wild pitches and passed balls.
3. Catchers frequently throw from the place where they retrieve the ball, instead of carrying the ball back to the plate before throwing it.
4. Pitchers frequently forget to cover home on a wild pitch or passed ball.

Consequently, this drill is as important for defensive reasons as it is for your offense.

## Practice with Runner on First and Third

Another situation drill that bears drilling is the "runner on first and third" situation, with fewer than two outs. On defense, we call it the "shortstop play." The purpose of the play is to make the runner on third think you are making a play at second and commit to starting home. The shortstop cuts off the catcher's throw to second and relays the ball back to the catcher to put the tag on the runner from third. When it works, it is beautiful to see, but it comes only with drilling. You must develop a signal between your catcher and shortstop without making it obvious to the other team that they are being set up. A good catcher/shortstop combination will do it with a look from the catcher and a tip of the cap by the shortstop to signal that he is ready.

## Hot Box Drill

Another situation drill that your boys will enjoy is the so-called "hot box drill," involving a runner trapped between bases. It happens often enough in Little League that taking the time to drill it periodically is justified. From the standpoint of offense, the runner should be coached to change directions and fake changing directions frequently to force more throws. If he can fake a change, making the fielder throw too soon, he will be safe every time. From the standpoint of defense, the opposite should be coached, i.e., to make as few throws as necessary and to chase the runner toward the base he came from, rather than the farther base. This is a play in which it is important to drill backup fielding. For example, on a trap between first and second, the first baseman and second baseman are the primary fielders. The pitcher backs up the first baseman, and the shortstop backs up the second baseman. If the runner gets by the primary fielder, the throw is made to the backup man, and the primary fielder quickly rolls out of the line of fire and becomes the backup man. The primary fielders on a trap between second and third are the shortstop and third baseman, and their backup men are the second baseman and the pitcher, respectively; between third and home, the primary fielders are the third baseman and the catcher, with the shortstop and pitcher their backup men, respectively. Note that the pitcher is involved as a backup man in every hot box play, which emphasizes the importance of having a savvy, good-fielding pitcher. Any time a fielder feels he can catch the runner before he reaches the base, he should try, rather than risk a throw. Only drilling will sharpen the skill and judgment of both runners and fielders in this situation.

## Throw Home Drill

One final "situation" that merits special practice is the "throw home drill." It involves a runner trying to score from third on a ground ball or after a fly ball or a runner trying to score from second on a hit to the outfield or to advance from second to third on a fly ball. You place the runner on base and, without letting the fielders know what to expect, hit a fly ball, a grounder, or a base hit to one of the outfielders. It is a good drill for teaching boys how to coach at third base, in addition to being a good offense/defense

Hot box drill: note first baseman has pitcher backing him up. Shortstop (out of picture) is backing up second baseman. Runner is being forced back to base he left.

drill. On the tag up on a fly ball, the runner should go into a sprint position, looking only at the next base, and the third base coach should act as his starter, giving him the "ready, set, go" signal vocally (and by hand signal to a runner on second). Some boys, despite drilling, never become aggressive enough in directing traffic as third base coaches, so when it's their turn to be a base coach, you just assign them to first base.

All of these situation drills will be fun for your boys, because each provides competition between the offense and defense, and there is nothing that will turn a dull practice into a fun practice faster than a little competition.

There are many other situation drills that could be organized, but with limited practice time available, you are well advised to concentrate on the basic situations that are likely to occur with some frequency during the course of a Little League season. Just remember that the formula for good, constructive practice sessions is: drill the basics, keep it simple, and make it fun!

# 9
# LETTING THEM ALL PLAY

One of the unique features of Little League baseball is the emphasis on letting *all players play.* In all other organized team competition, only the best players play, and the rest "warm the bench." Playing everyone is not only encouraged by Little League; it is written into the rules.

When my former co-manager, Jim Williams, and I started coaching together in our local league, our sons Jim and Paul, respectively, were 8 years old. We took on the management of a Minor League team and had 20 players—boys and girls—on the squad. So we instituted a 20-player batting order to give every player an *equal* opportunity to bat, and we rotated freely in the field. Despite some grumbling from several gung ho Minor League managers, this "equal opportunity to play" policy was adopted as a rule in our league on the basis that instruction and experience are the major objectives in Minor League baseball (Little League headquarters has published a leaflet on T-Ball that also encourages informality, instruction, and total participation for Minor League baseball.)

Two years later, Jim Williams and I moved up to Little League with our two sons—the third time in 15 years that I had made that

116

trip up with each of my respective sons. Of course we knew that full-squad batting orders and unrestricted substitutions were too informal for Little League, but we also knew that the concept of participation by all players was preserved.

In taking a boy from age 6 to age 15 through three levels of competition—Minor League to Little League to Senior League— the Little League rules provide a gradual transition from the equal opportunity to play in Minor League, to the guaranteed but not equal opportunity to play in Little League, to the "play if you're good enough, ride the bench if you're not" opportunity to play in Senior League. Little League straddles the best of both worlds; it assures every boy that *he will play* in every game, but says that *how much he will play* depends on his ability and hustle. The 9- or 10-year-old rookie will probably play only the mandatory two innings; the 12-year-old All Star will probably play all six innings. When I hear a rookie complain about not playing enough, I suggest that he ask his teammate, the 12-year-old All Star, how much he played when he was a rookie. A rookie gets his first exposure to the facts of life of having to compete for a position on the team but still has the fun of playing some and feeling a part of the team. And he knows that he will play more in subsequent seasons—if he hustles!

In Little League, there are two rules that guarantee every player an opportunity to play in every game:

*Regulation IV (i):* "Every player on a team roster will participate in each game for a minimum of six (6) defensive outs and bat at least one time."

*Rule 3.03:* "A player in the starting lineup who has been removed for a substitute may reenter the game once, in any position in the batting order, provided:
1. The substitute has completed one time at bat and
2. has played defensively for a minimum of six (6) consecutive outs.
3. A pitcher may not reenter the game as pitcher.
4. Only a player in the starting lineup may reenter the game."

Those two provisions, guaranteeing that every player will play and allowing starting players to reenter the game, are unique in organized sports. They speak well of the founders of Little League baseball, who put such a high premium on the importance of giving every child an opportunity to play.

Unfortunately, it is possible for a manager to implement these rules to the letter but ignore the spirit of letting every boy play. A new manager should understand the loopholes and be prepared to object if he feels another manager is abusing the spirit of the rule. For example, the manager of the visiting team, which is losing 6–4, could wait to insert his worst player in the lineup until the defensive half of the fifth inning and put him in a batting position that would have him hitting last. If the score didn't change, the substitute could play only one defensive inning since the home team wouldn't bat in the bottom of the sixth, and he would not get up to bat. The only way the manager could possibly fulfill the mandatory playing requirements for that boy, within six innings, would be for his team to tie the game or go ahead in the top of the sixth and send at least nine batters to the plate! Yet the manager could argue that he followed the letter of the rule by putting in the substitute for the last two innings. The boy had the *possibility* of meeting the mandatory requirements, but not the *probability,* and the manager obviously violated the spirit of the rule. Unfortunately, it happens, but when a manager does it, I have trouble understanding how he can look the boy in the eye when both of them know that he was supposed to have played two innings and batted once.

In order to provide some assurance that managers live up to the spirit of the mandatory playing rule, our local league, after some managerial abuse of the spirit of the rule, passed a local regulation that requires all substitutes to enter the game by no later than the defensive half of the fourth inning. Every player would then be assured of his minimum six consecutive outs in the field, although mathematically it would still be possible for him not to bat, e.g., if he was on the visiting team and entered the game defensively in the bottom of the fourth. With only two innings in which to bat, if only six boys go to the plate in the fifth and sixth, and he was to have batted seventh, eighth, or ninth, he would not bat. However, that would be a rare situation, and it would be obvious that the manager intended to abide by the rule. To guarantee absolutely that a substitute would meet the mandatory playing requirements, a local league would have to rule that all substitutes be put into the game before the fourth inning, and I understand there are leagues that have adopted such a local rule.

Our local league, acting on the penalty note at the end of Regulation IV (i), established penalties that have virtually erased the violations of the mandatory playing rule. The first violation carries a written censure and requires the manager to insert the boy (who was deprived from playing) in the starting lineup of the following game and allow him to play four innings in the field and bat twice before he can be removed. The second violation will result in the suspension of the manager for a specified period. The third violation will result in his dismissal as a manager.

It is not just enough for a manager to get all of his substitutes *into* the game on a timely basis; he may not *remove* them from the game, once inserted, until they have met the mandatory playing requirement. Under Rule 3.03, the manager may not reinsert a starter until his substitute has batted once and played six consecutive outs in the field. For example, Billy Jones starts the game and is replaced in the third inning by Tommy Brown. The manager may plan to play Tommy only two innings and put starter Billy back in the game in the fifth. However, if his team goes up and down in order in the third and fourth innings, and Tommy was not one of the six boys who batted, he would have to remain in the game for another inning and Billy could not reenter. If Billy was a star player, there would be a real temptation for the manager to put him back in the game, perhaps substituting him for another boy who *has* played the mandatory time, but if he did, he would be violating Rule 3.03. The situation can be further complicated by the fact that a substitute may replace one player in the batting order but another in the field if two substitutes enter the game at the same time. With both starters leaving the game at the same time, there may be some confusion as to which one has to stay out until his substitute fulfills the mandatory playing requirements. The player he replaced in the batting order has to remain out, but who is going to check that?

I don't believe you can depend on the official scorer to audit the comings and goings of 12 possible substitutes and their replacements for the two teams, since not only will he be busy keeping the scorebook, but in many cases he will not be knowledgeable enough about the rules to be able to spot the violation. A conscientious umpire may keep track, but most do not. So I keep track by charting the other team's substitutions. In conformance with Rules 3.06 and 3.07, I ask the manager of the other team and the umpire-in-chief to advise me of all substitutions. I recommend that you keep a record of the opposing team's substitutions in the dugout scorebook, for two reasons. First, from a game strategy stand-point, you would know *whom* the opposing team is substituting, *when,* and at *what position,* so you can advise your team of possible weaknesses that have been introduced to the other team. For example, a new catcher would encourage more daring base running; you might want to test a new outfielder's arm by stretching a single into a double; or your pitcher should be advised of a weak pinch hitter so he can pitch to him accordingly. (More will be said about this in Chapter 11.) I keep a record of the opposing team's substitutions so I can relay this information to my team, but it also serves to keep the opposing manager honest in adhering to the mandatory playing rule.

A new manager should also be aware of another potential inequity that can be foisted on him by an opposing manager who doesn't abide by the spirit of the substitution rule. He can put you at a disadvantage by bringing a smaller squad to the game than you have. If your league calls for a 15-player roster, and you have 15 players for a game, but the opposing manager shows up with only 12, you are obviously at a 3-player disadvantage from the standpoint of the mandatory playing rule, since he can play his starters longer than you can. It is understandable that sickness, vacations, and other legitimate reasons will occasionally prevent players from showing up, but when a manager consistently shows up with players missing, you have to be suspicious that he is violating Regulation III (d), which requires him to take prompt action to fill vacancies in his roster, and your player agent should be alerted. Not only is that manager cheating your team, but he is also depriving boys from playing who should be filling out his roster. One such manager in our league showed up for a game with our team with only 11 players, something he had done previously to several other teams. As fate would have it, 3 of his players were injured in the game, and he had to forfeit the game for failure to field a 9-man team in the fourth inning (Rule 4.17). It was poetic justice, and he showed up with a full squad after that.

I also make up a chart for *our* team before each game, showing both the defensive lineup and the batting order for each inning. It lets every boy know what position he will play, when he will play it, and where he will bat in the batting order. I make several copies and post them in the dugout so the players on our team will be able to anticipate every defensive and offensive change affecting them. I also give a copy of the chart to the official scorekeeper, advising him to note the lineup changes when they occur, but I reserve the right to change the chart if the situation demands it.

With Rule 3.03 permitting a starting player to reenter the game, but only if his substitute has played his mandatory two innings in the field and batted once, some recordkeeping is necessary to keep track of the ins and outs of the starters and the substitutes. I prefer to do my recordkeeping before the fact on a chart so I don't have to worry about it during the game or trust my memory to make sure all boys get the proper opportunity to play.

In the next chapter, Figure 4 shows an example of a hypothetical chart that I might use, listing both defensive and offensive lineups of my team on one page. I also schedule the base coaches—an assignment your substitutes will enjoy *almost* as much as playing.

From a game strategy standpoint, some thought must be given to the question of when to insert the substitutes and still maintain a good balance of experienced and inexperienced players. That is another good reason for charting your substitutes in advance, rather than playing it by ear. The latter could result in your discovering in the fourth inning that you have to insert all of your substitutes at once—with the score tied.

Some managers prefer to put all of their substitutes in early and be done with it. There is some merit in this since it would give you the assurance of having your strongest team for the last innings and also give you the opportunity to let your substitutes reenter the game (assuming they started) if the score is lopsided in the final innings. The danger in doing this is the possibility of allowing the other team to get an early lead against your weak players. This forces you to play catch-up ball, which can be both a psychological and a real disadvantage. I prefer to stagger my substitutes. The reasoning behind this will be explained in Chapter 11.

# 10

# HANDLING PARENTS AND PRESSURE

It is appropriate to treat two of the most controversial subjects in Little League—parents and pressure—in the same chapter, because to a degree there is a cause-and-effect relationship between the two.

## HANDLING PARENTS

In a close Little League tournament game in our town several years ago, the visiting team was trailing 5–4 at the end of the fifth inning but rallied to score three runs in the top of the sixth. However, in doing so, they consumed so much time that the umpires were forced to call the game on account of darkness in the middle of the sixth. Consequently, the score reverted to the standing at the end of the fifth inning, and the other team won! The umpires' judgment was correct, and the rule is clear, but the boys on the losing team were in tears, and the tirade that ensued by their parents against the umpires was not to be believed! I have an unforgettable recollection of the head umpire finally saying to one of our leading citizens (whose son was on the losing team), "It is parents like you who ruin Little League for the kids!"

I have seen intelligent, well-educated *fathers and mothers* lose all sense of reason in a Little League dispute involving their children. I have seen a father pull his son off the bench and off the team because the manager did not start him in a game. I have seen a manager quit because his son was not picked for the All Star team (by the players of the league). I have seen former friends stop talking because of Little League disputes involving their children. And worst of all, I have seen too many cases of parents pressuring their children to perform at a level they were incapable of reaching.

A friend of mine who umpires in another league told the sad story of such a father who berated his son every time he struck out or made an error. In one game, the boy had struck out once and taken his father's public tirade. On his second time at bat, with the bases loaded, he got caught looking at a third strike, and the umpire called him out again. In utter frustration and anticipation of what he would get from his father, the boy turned on the umpire and swung his bat across his chest protector. Naturally, the umpire threw him out of the game, but he wished there had been some punishment he could have meted out to the father as well.

In our local league, parental abuse got so bad that our league president had to write a letter, shown in Figure 3, warning parents that they could be asked to leave the park or could cause the forfeiture of a game if they did not control themselves.

What causes some normal, law-abiding parents to become such rabid, irrational hotheads over a Little League game? It is human nature for parents to view their children through somewhat biased eyes, and when their son or daughter gets hurt, they get angry! The tears come easily to 9- to 12-year-old children, and what parent does not react protectively when he sees his child crying and hurt, emotionally or physically?

I use the word *child* advisedly, because I think the fact that 9- to 12-year-olds are still children is symptomatic of the problem; the younger the child, the more the parent is protective and defensive of him or her. And when the child is hurt or unhappy, the parent looks for someone to blame: if the child struck out, the umpire is the culprit; if he or she doesn't play enough, the manager is unfair! The fact that the age of Little Leaguers is significant is confirmed by the observation that the problem doesn't arise in the Senior League, where the boys are older, more independent, and less dependent on or desirous of the protection of Mom and Dad.

How do you cope with the parent problem? I believe *communications* and *control* are the key words.

A good program of communications with parents, at both the league level and the team level, will create the kind of positive atmosphere that will eliminate most of the problems with parents and other fans at games. However, a league is well advised to have a policy of control—well understood by managers, coaches, umpires, and league officers—to deal with fan abuse when it occurs. (If it has never occurred in your league, you are a rare exception and should count your blessings.)

The manager and coaches of a team should be responsible for controlling the behavior of their fans, as well as their players. Sometimes, however, they are guilty of inciting them rather than controlling them. In such cases, control of the manager and coaches should be exercised by the president of the league, who has that authority. It is sometimes difficult for those closely involved in a game to keep proper perspective. That's why the Little League rules wisely require a league president to be uninvolved with any team in the league, so he can be impartial in bringing matters back into proper perspective if they get out of line.

The umpires, appointed by the president, have the responsibility of keeping matters under control on the playing field and have the authority, as pointed out in the letter quoted in Figure 3, to remove fans (parents or others) from the stands if they get out of control.

Education of the parents begins in your Minor League organization, where the children are the youngest and the parents are therefore inclined to be the most protective. Just when our league felt we had the parental situation under control, and our umpires and coaches had established excellent rapport, our Minor League organization asked us to provide umpires for their All Star game (which itself is contrary to the instruction philosophy of Minor League play). Our umpires soon realized how much we had accomplished in Little League when they were subjected to the unfair abuse of both coaches and parents. It became clear to our league that we needed some reeducation at the Minor League level, or the same parents (and possibly coaches) would be reintroducing a blight that we thought had been cured as they moved up to Little League.

Many of the problems with parents are caused by a lack of

## FIGURE 3.

TO:   Parents and Fans of Summersville Little League

Critics of Little League baseball often say that poor sportsmanship on the part of the parents ruins the program for the children. Unfortunately, the conduct of a few parents has created a situation that must and will be corrected.

The children on the field want and need the support of their fans. Such support should always be in the form of positive encouragement to the players. No fan should criticize umpires, managers, or players of either team. Again, all cheering should be directed to the team that you are supporting. Fans will abide by the same rules that apply to players regarding their conduct; example: Rule 4.06 (2), "No manager, coach, player, or fan shall, at any time, whether from the bench or elsewhere, use language that will in any manner refer to or reflect upon opposing players, umpires, or coaches." I am instructing all umpires to take the following action to control fan abuse:

(1)   Any parent or fan who voices strong and persistent displeasure with an umpire's decision or who loudly criticizes any player will be first warned by the umpire(s).

(2)   If such acts are flagrant or are repeated, the fan will be asked to leave the park.

(3)   If a parent refuses to comply with the umpire's request, the umpire will suspend for the duration of the game the son or daughter he or she is supporting, and both will be asked to leave.

(4)   In extreme cases, the umpire may cause the game to be forfeited to the offended team.

Hopefully, this letter will serve to remind all fans that Little League is simply a game, a game played with a ball and little children. Conduct displayed at higher levels of play will not be tolerated in Little League.

Sincerely,

James M. Richmond
President
Summersville Little League

understanding; thus the importance of communications. For example, the parent of a boy who was in the Minor League last year and played on an equal time basis with all other players doesn't understand why his boy plays only two innings and bats only once this year in Little League. The parent and son are both new to Little League, and if someone doesn't explain the rules, the parent can be forgiven for being confused. Don't count on the boy to interpret the rules for his parents; youngsters of ages 9–12 are notorious for not taking information—or at least the right information—home to their parents. Ask any teacher.

I use the teacher's proven formula for communicating with parents: sending notes home. All it takes is a typewriter, a photocopying machine, and a little time. But the time will be well invested in the parental support it will generate and the parental problems it will prevent. Parents will range in behavior from those who look over your shoulder to those you never see, and each extreme creates its own set of potential problems for the manager.

The first time I recommend a written communication between the manager and the parents is when their son is drafted. I know of several cases in which a boy and his parents assumed that being drafted by a team, after going through registration and tryouts, meant the boy had made that team. You can understand the trauma that occurred when he got home one night and tried to explain to his parents that he had just been cut. I think it is important to explain to parents, new to Little League, what it is all about, and specifically to let them know what their son should expect. Since most 9-year-old boys are cut, as well as many who are 10, it is important to prepare both the boy and his parents for this eventuality—in a positive way.

The kind of letter I use after the draft is shown on the next page (Figure 3A).

The wording of the letter may not be appropriate for every league and team, but the important thing is to let the boy and his parents know what will be happening. One of the best ways to get the cooperation of parents is to ask them to help. Some of the most dedicated parents I have had the pleasure of working with might never have become involved if they hadn't been given the opportunity to volunteer. A lot of people who would be willing to help are reticent to take the first step to volunteer. I create as many official jobs as I can: coaches, scorekeeper, equipment manager, team mother, telephone committee (if you don't think you need one, wait until the first rainy day when 15 boys call you to find out if the game is on). We also ask all mothers to help by taking a turn providing the "dugout drinks" at each practice and game. (Boys get thirsty during practice and games.) Your league can always use

## FIGURE 3A.

Dear Parent:

Your son has been drafted to try out for my Little League baseball team, the Giants. We have eight openings on our team, and your son will be competing for one of those positions. It is tough for a boy to make the team the first time he is drafted, especially if he is only nine years old. But he is guaranteed the opportunity to play on a team--if not a Little League team, then a Minor League team--as long as he tries hard and is faithful about coming to practice.

Our team coaches and I are volunteers who also have boys in Little League. We will be devoting a lot of time to the boys on our team, and we ask you to help your son in two important ways:

1. Get him to and from practice and games on time;

2. Encourage him in every way possible, including practicing with him at home, if you can.

On the enclosed sheet are the names and phone numbers of all of the boys who were drafted by the Giants and the returning Giants. You may want to plan a car pool with some others who live near you. The practice schedule is also listed on the attached sheet; practice is always held at the Little League field in Memorial Park.

Your son will be told before April 15 whether he has been selected to play for the Giants or, if not, to what team he has been assigned.

If you have any questions, please feel free to call me at 872-4651; or call Fred Roberts, the player agent who is responsible for assigning players to teams, at 872-3502.

Sincerely,


Ned McIntosh
Giants Manager

volunteer ground keepers, umpires, parents to work in the concession stand, etc.

By finding out what tasks parents would like to take on, you can avoid an embarrassing situation that happened to me in asking dads to help. I noticed a dad watching practice, and none of my coaches had shown up yet, so I asked him to hit fly balls to our outfielders. The poor fellow had never played baseball as a boy and was totally uncoordinated. He tried, but it was embarrassing for him and his son. I converted him to our official scorekeeper and statistician, and he did a super job in an important assignment that he was capable of handling. I now talk to the interested dads and find out how they would like to help, rather than throwing them into an embarrassing situation.

The second time I recommend a formal communication with parents is just before the season opens. At this point you will have made your draft cuts and selected the boys (and their parents) with whom you will be spending a great deal of time for the next quarter of a year. On this occasion I recommend a parents' meeting rather than just a letter. To be sure of a full attendance, I tell the boys we will pass out their game uniforms and league schedules at the meeting. I tell them to assure their parents the meeting will be brief, so rather than drop them off and come back to get them, they may as well stay.

At the meeting, I pass out the team schedule (Figure 4), which shows next to each date the dugout drinks assignment; the team roster (Figure 5); and the telephone committee call sequence (Figure 5). I suggest the parents post both sheets in a conspicuous spot at home. I hold the meeting in a central location (usually in a church meeting room) and keep my promise to make it brief. But I plan some light refreshments to encourage those who want to stay and visit. It is revealing in such an informal session to hear how many misconceptions about Little League exist, and this meeting may give you an opportunity to set them straight.

The only other scheduled get-together we hold is a team picnic at the end of the year, which the mothers arrange. Since parents and coaches got acquainted and started communicating early in the season, and continued during the season, by picnic time we are old friends with a good rapport. With all of your attempts to communicate and establish good rapport, you may still have to deal with parents who are unreasonable in their bias. A friend of mine who is a high school coach told me how discouraging it is for him to deal with parents who are so selfish that they would rather have their boys play and the team lose than have them ride the bench and have the team win. I encountered an extreme case, which illustrates how biased some parents can be about their children. I took out five of our regular players and replaced them with five substitutes when our team got off to a lopsided lead. The mother of one of the regulars challenged me after the game about why I had taken her son out of the game. I was surprised at the question since her son had played nearly all innings of all games, but I reminded her that we had a big lead and I wanted to give the substitutes a chance to play. She then asked why I had taken *her* son out but left another particular player in. I then realized that her bias was so strong that she was not satisfied unless her son was treated as the *best* player on the team.

On another occasion, a mother who was watching our practice got very upset when one of my coaches criticized her boy (for good reason). She was so sensitive that she overreacted to *anyone's* criticizing her son. The coach took her aside and explained that, when the boys are on the field, it is the coach's responsibility to criticize a boy who does something wrong, just as it is a parent's responsibility to do the same at home.

These examples merely underscore the fact that parents cannot be objective about their own children, and your best efforts to establish a proper attitude with your players will sometimes be undermined by their own parents. It would be unrealistic to expect to eliminate all parental bias; the best you can do is to minimize it by establishing good communications and setting a good example, which is a challenge to your objectivity when your own child is on your team.

So much for handling parents; now we turn to handling pressure!

## FIGURE 4. GIANTS SCHEDULE, SUMMERSVILLE LITTLE LEAGUE

| Day | Date | Time | Opponent | Home or Visitors | Dugout Drinks |
|-----|------|------|----------|------------------|---------------|
| Saturday | April 25 | 6:00 P.M. | Reds | V | Cox |
| Monday | April 27 | 6:00 P.M. | Nettie Astros | H | Beirne |
| Wednesday | April 29 | 7:30 P.M. | Pirates | V | Girod |
| Monday | May 4 | 6:00 P.M. | Hawks | H | Hoard |
| Wednesday | May 6 | 7:30 P.M. | Birch River | V | Walton |
| Tuesday | May 12 | 7:30 P.M. | Yankees | H | Grose |
| Thursday | May 14 | 6:00 P.M. | Cubs | V | Acree |
| Tuesday | May 19 | 6:00 P.M. | Cardinals | V | Williams |
| Friday | May 22 | 6:00 P.M. | Nettie Rangers | H | Joo |

### END OF FIRST HALF

| Day | Date | Time | Opponent | Home or Visitors | Dugout Drinks |
|-----|------|------|----------|------------------|---------------|
| Monday | May 25 | 7:30 P.M. | Nettie Astros | V | Blankenship |
| Wednesday | May 27 | 6:00 P.M. | Pirates | H | Proctor |
| Monday | June 1 | 7:30 P.M. | Hawks | V | Lipscomb |
| Wednesday | June 3 | 6:00 P.M. | Birch River | H | Cox |
| Tuesday | June 9 | 6:00 P.M. | Yankees | V | Beirne |
| Thursday | June 11 | 7:30 P.M. | Cubs | H | Girod |
| Tuesday | June 16 | 7:30 P.M. | Cardinals | H | Hoard |
| Friday | June 19 | 7:30 P.M. | Nettie Rangers | V | Thomas |
| Wednesday | June 24 | 6:00 P.M. | Reds | H | McIntosh |

## FIGURE 5. GIANTS ROSTER

| Name | Telephone |
|---|---|
| Lane Acree | 555-1579 |
| Jim Beirne | 555-3097 |
| Rod Blankenship | 555-5218 |
| Rodney Cox | 555-3345 |
| Jeff Girod | 555-3422 |
| Mike Grose | 555-5355 |
| John Hoard | 555-6686 |
| David Joo | 555-2793 |
| Mike Lipscomb | 555-4923 |
| Jim McIntosh | 555-4651 |
| Mark Proctor | 555-5777 |
| Chuck Thomas | 555-6392 |
| Mike Walton | 555-5847 |
| Paul Williams | 555-5384 |

## TELEPHONE COMMITTEE

| McIntosh | calls | Acree | who calls | Beirne Blankenship Grose |
|---|---|---|---|---|
| McIntosh | calls | Cox | who calls | Girod Lipscomb Walton |
| McIntosh | calls | Hoard | who calls | Joo Proctor Thomas Williams |

## HANDLING PRESSURE

There is no way to remove pressure from competitive sports; it's inherent in the fact that each team is trying to beat the other, and inevitably there will be tense, pressure-packed game situations. The Little League player is exposed to pressure when he comes to bat with the bases loaded and the tying run on third, and his teammates, coaches, and parents are imploring him to "do it!" ("Come on, Charlie, you can do it!") If he strikes out, you'll hear the critics say how awful it was to subject the poor kid to all that pressure. If he hits a home run, nobody mentions the pressure, except possibly someone on the other side, who may say how awful it was to subject that poor pitcher to all that pressure!

Elimination of the pressure is impossible, so the best that you can accomplish as a coach is to keep it in proper perspective and handle it sensitively, keeping in mind that you are dealing with children. It's when the coaches and/or the parents lose the proper perspective that the pressure problem becomes acute.

In saying that all athletic competition puts pressure on the players, it is important again to point out that Little League baseball differs from all other athletic competition. "Winning is everything" is the Vince Lombardi philosophy of competitive athletics, and many team coaches openly and/or actually handle their players and teams according to that philosophy. Little League baseball is unique among competitive sports in encouraging a counterphilosophy to "winning is everything," namely, "the boy comes first." The fact that Little League does not subscribe to the "winning is everything" philosophy is implicit in its rules, e.g., the mandatory playing rule that guarantees that all boys get an opportunity to play in each game, the pitching limitation rule that restricts the number of innings per week a boy may pitch, the rule limiting the number of 12-year-olds a team may have on its roster, the rule that limits the number of 12-year-olds who can pitch in a week, etc. If "winning is everything" were the philosophy of Little League, then rules like these, restricting the use of the best players, which in turn restricts the opportunity to win, would not have been written. The manager who criticizes these restrictive rules or tries to circumvent them is acting in basic opposition to Little League principles.

The late Dr. Arthur A. Esslinger said it best in the *Little League Baseball Official Regulations and Playing Rules:*

> The heart of Little League Baseball is what happens between manager and boy. It is your manager more than any other single individual who makes your program a success or failure. He controls the situation in which players may be benefited or harmed. We have all seen managers who exerted a wonderful influence upon their boys—an influence which was as fine an educational experience as any lad might undergo. Unfortunately, we have also observed a few managers who were a menace to children.

In his last reference, we think Dr. Esslinger may have had in mind the Little League manager who handles children according to the "winning is everything" philosophy.

Pressure is inevitable in a Little League game, and helping a child expect it, accept it, and handle it constructively can be a coach's contribution to the maturing process that helps make a child an adult. Yet it is a challenge to a manager's dedication to the "boy comes first" philosophy when he sees one of his boys blow a key play that loses a game or sees another strike out when a hit would have won a game. If the manager can empathize, rather than criticize, he has the right perspective.

The worst example I have seen of an insensitive manager's mishandling a boy's mistake under pressure occurred in a recent district All Star game. The score was tied, the bases were loaded, and there were two outs in the bottom of the third. The batter hit an easy ground ball to the second baseman, who had a sure third out at first. But the second baseman obviously thought there was only one out, so he threw home to force the lead runner and missed. His reaction showed that he immediately realized what he had done wrong. To add insult to injury, however, his manager called time and pulled him out of the game, to the complete humiliation of the boy in front of his teammates, parents, and friends. Ironically, the substitute the manager put in at second base booted an easy ground ball on the very next play, which only served to underscore the callous way the manager had handled a child's mistake under pressure.

The application of the sound principle "praise in public, criticize in private" is key to the sensitive handling of children who are getting their first taste of competitive pressure, and it should be used not only by the manager and coaches but by teammates and parents as well. And since we are dealing with children not used to the pressures of competitive athletics, I would recommend going "the second mile" and finding something encouraging to say to a boy when he doesn't perform well under pressure. My favorite technique is the "sandwich method" of constructive criticism; i.e., sandwich two compliments on either side of a criticism. For example, the infielder who throws wild to first base could be told, "You were right on your toes in getting in front of that ground ball, Joey, and you fielded it well, but you rushed your throw to first. You keep up the good work on fielding the ball, and we'll work more with you on your throws to first." To the boy who strikes out, you might say, "That was a good level swing, Jim, but you were out in front of the ball. Glad you're in there swinging, though, so we'll work on your timing in practice." In both cases, you have removed the sting of failure, restored some pride, and given the players something encouraging to look forward to.

Fear—either fear of failure or fear of being hurt—is the principal source of pressure. One is emotional, the other physical, and both of them are very real. Fear of failing his teammates, his parents, and his coaches and the related fear of the pride-shattering ridicule he may be subjected to in school—and, unfortunately, sometimes even from his parents and coaches—is a fear, if realized, that can make Little League a miserable experience instead of a fun one.

The fear of being hurt is no less frightening to a young player unaccustomed to the speed of a ball thrown by a big 12-year-old. The range in size and physical development between the biggest 12-year-old and the smallest 9-year-old in your league underscores the potential danger that exists, in addition to the psychological fear, when the smaller boy steps up to the plate to face the bigger one. A coach must be careful to help the rookie adjust gradually to the higher level of play, or he could be physically hurt and/or become emotionally gun-shy at the plate. If the young player does actually get hit by a hard-thrown ball—and it happens—the coach has the special challenge of reconditioning that boy to batting without letting fear interfere with his concentration.

"The boy comes first" philosophy requires the coach to recognize the individual differences and needs of each boy on his team. The boys are all at different stages of development, physically and in terms of ability, and therefore their levels of achievement are different. For example, two hits in a game may be routine for your 12-year-old All Star player but would be a banner achievement for your youngest rookie. In motivating our players, while recognizing these individual differences, we adopted a version of the "Stargell's Stars" made famous by Willie Stargell of the Pittsburgh Pirates. Our stars are inexpensive felt stars (about 2¢ each), in the team color that contrasts with the solid cap color (orange on black). After each game, we award a star for something a boy did in that game that was exceptional *for him at his ability and development level.* A rookie would get a star for getting his first hit or for making a fielding play that was good *for him* (which might be routine for an experienced player). Naturally, before the season is very old, we manage to find something that is worthy of at least one star for every boy on the team. Talk about motivation; you would think those inexpensive felt stars were made of gold the way the boys work for them! And talk about pride; you should see how quickly they have their mothers sew them on their caps!

The first season that we used our "Stargell Stars," our team won both the league championship and the county championship. However, one of the opposing managers apparently thought there must have been a cause-and-effect relationship, because he objected to our using them the next season. He said it intimidated his batters to face our pitchers with their star-studded caps. His objection was proper, since it pointed up our technical violation of Rule 1, 11, which says all uniforms must be identical, so we abandoned the use of the stars for our game caps. However, the coaches and I felt so strongly about the motivational value of the stars that we bought our players a set of practice caps and told them to have their mothers sew the stars on *them*. And it worked just as effectively, because they wore their star-studded caps to school, as well as to practice, which still gave them special recognition. We won the league and county championships again the next year, so the stars on the caps apparently did not represent a cause-and-effect relationship. Their motivational and morale value, however, convinced the coaches and me that they were worth their weight in gold.

It is important to explain that we sometimes give out "Stargell Stars" when our team loses and conversely may not give them out when our team wins. For instance, a boy could earn a star for an outstanding performance in a losing game; on the other hand, we could beat a weak team, as expected, without any outstanding performances by individual players. And when we win a big game, and it has been a team effort, we sometimes give a star to every boy on the team. It's the special effort, the extra hustle that wins the recognition, not just the game score.

When you ignore the "winning is everything" philosophy and substitute recognition of a boy, based on his personal level of ability, you defuse some of the pressure caused by the fear of failure. You are telling a boy that success in Little League is not measured just in terms of the game score but also in terms of his

Opposing coaches claimed our pitcher's star-studded cap intimidated the batters.

hustle. If he hustles more, he will surely help the team more, and if all the players keep hustling more, the team is bound to improve. And those are our measurements of personal and team success!

Fortunately, boys accept this philosophy of success more easily than do their coaches and parents, who in many cases have been conditioned by the "winning is everything" philosophy in adult competitive sports. Little League is different—different in a better way for children in their formative years of exposure to competitive sports—and perhaps Little League's greatest challenge lies in teaching this to the adults.

# 11
# WINNING

The old adage "I've been rich and I've been poor, but being rich is better" could apply to winning and losing, too. It's just plain more fun to win. You've heard the philosophy "No coach can win unless he has the material to work with." That's generally true in sports, but in my opinion it's less true in Little League baseball than in any other sport that I can think of. You've also heard it said that "There is very little a coach can do to affect the outcome of a game." Not true in Little League, in my judgment. Little League managers and coaches can contribute a great deal to whether they build a winning or a losing team; the only question is whether they are willing and able to take the necessary time and make the necessary effort. In some cases, they may be putting in enough time but not planning it intelligently.

Throughout this entire book, we have been developing a winning philosophy, without calling it such, which is made up of:

- teaching the basics;
- drilling the basics; and
- making it fun!

If there is one single factor, above all, that will affect the success of your team it will be the amount of time you are willing and able to spend with your boys on following that "winning formula." Perhaps the most satisfying year I spent as a manager was a year we *didn't* win a championship; we came in third in a 10-team league. It was after we had won the league and county championships twice, back to back, and we had very little returning material to build on. We had graduated eight 12-year-old starters, including four All Star players, had only two 11-year-olds coming up, had last pick in the draft, and had to pick eight rookies from a crop of prospects that was generally considered weak. One of the finest compliments I received as a manager came from a fellow manager who said at the end of that season, "If we had a Manager of the Year award, you should have won it for starting the year with a team that had absolutely nothing but finished in third place." In all of my years in coaching Little League baseball, I have never had a team that did not have a winning season, so the "winning formula" has apparently been effective.

It's a copout for a manager or coach to say that there is very little he can do to influence his team's success. In addition to his indirect contribution to a winning team through teaching and drilling the basics, there are some direct contributions he can make in the areas of coaching strategy.

## CHOOSING YOUR PLAYERS

If you believe that "no coach can win unless he has the material to work with," then you should carefully reread Chapter 1, "Choosing Your Players." Since the material you work with is selected by you in the player draft, the responsibility is yours to do a thorough job of scouting the prospects prior to the draft. If you end up with the worst material in the draft, whose fault is it but yours? One year when I had last pick in the draft, I got the boy who was generally considered the best pick. How? By drafting his dad as my coach. It was all done in accordance with the rules. I had lost my two coaches, whose sons graduated into the Senior League, so I had a legitimate opening for a coach. The rule (in the president's manual) says, "If a team has more than one coach, only the senior coach may qualify (to claim his son), provided that senior member has served as a coach in the league for two or more years. If the senior coach does not have sons and/or daughters, the coach next in seniority may exercise the privilege." The coach I picked had been his son's manager for two years in our organization's Minor League and was hoping to have the opportunity to continue coaching his son in Little League. There were three Minor League coaches who were in the same situation, but, fortunately for our team, the best coach available was also the father of the best draft pick. It required some research on my part to determine the facts, just as it requires some research to get a line on all of the eligible draft choices. As mentioned in Chapter 1, your boys will be your best scouts. If a new kid has moved to town, and your boys tell you how good he is at kickball during school recess, chances are that he is a physically strong boy with some natural athletic ability; in short, a good draft prospect.

## COACHING YOUR PITCHERS

As we mentioned in Chapter 7, "The Basics of Pitching," most Little League coaches will agree that having a winning team is more than 50 percent dependent on having good pitching. Yet most of the same managers will spend less than 10 percent of total practice time working with their pitchers. They will also tell you about how many games they lost because of walks, but they don't connect that fact with practice time they have failed to spend on their pitchers' control.

### Pitching Practice

I believe a pitcher must have hours of extra practice, besides regular team practice, especially on perfecting his control. This is what I meant in saying that a winning team may depend most on how much time a coach is willing and able to devote to it. The child who is really dedicated to becoming a good pitcher *will* be willing and able to devote the time. But he needs a parent, older sibling, or coach to work with him. Don't be naive enough to think that unsupervised youngsters will practice as long or as effectively as they will with a coach. Fortunately, you don't need a full baseball diamond to practice pitching. I built a backstop out of two-by-fours and chicken wire, a plate and pitcher's rubber out of wood, and a pitcher's mound out of fill dirt—all in my backyard.

As mentioned in Chapter 7, always have a batter when your

When your pitcher is warming up before the game starts, always have a batter in the batter's box to give your pitcher the proper perspective.

pitchers and catchers are working out. He should wear a helmet, take practice swings and fake bunts, but not hit the ball. Both a pitcher and a catcher must get used to working under the most realistic conditions possible. Be sure to teach your pitcher how to pitch from the set position. Many coaches do not teach it, since leading off base is not allowed in Little League. However, it is a legal position, and I have found that a pitcher who is having control problems will improve his control by foregoing the windup and just throwing the ball from the set position, particularly when he is pitching to the lower half of the batting order.

## Warming Up

One important observation about Little League pitchers on the day they pitch: they generally don't warm up enough. They aren't really warmed up until they break into a sweat, but most will stop short of that, thinking that they are overdoing it when they start to perspire. I have seen too many pitchers get off to a shaky start because they had not warmed up enough; significantly, many settle down after a lot of walks and hits because the walks and hits became their warm-ups.

## Preventing Sore Arms

Another important observation is that pitchers do not take care of their arms unless you coach them to do so. I always insist that my pitchers wear a three-quarter-length shirt under their game jerseys, and that they bring jackets. When they have warmed up, they should put on the jacket, wear it in the dugout between innings, and wear it on base when they are running bases. If Major League pitchers do this to keep their pitching arms from getting stiff, why shouldn't it be just as important for Little League pitchers? Most cases of sore arms I have encountered were not a result of too much supervised practice but of too much unsupervised practice. I have had a boy report on the day he was supposed to pitch in a 7:30 P.M. game, complaining about a sore arm. The truth finally came out that he had been playing "burnout" (seeing how hard they could throw the ball to each other) with some other boys after school.

## Scheduling Pitchers

Scheduling your pitchers is definitely an area in which managerial skill can contribute to a team's success. The rules regarding rest between pitching assignments must be understood thoroughly. I can recall an instance in which I contributed to our team's losing an important game by not remembering the pitching rules. We had two games in a week, on Tuesday and Thursday, with the Thursday game being the more difficult of the two. I started my number one pitcher in the Tuesday game, and after two innings we had built a good lead, so I took him out so he would have four innings' eligibility on Thursday. We won the game, and everything would have been fine, except that it rained on Thursday, and the game was rescheduled for Saturday. So on Saturday, I pitched our number one pitcher four innings and our number two pitcher two innings in a close game, since that was the eligibility each had remaining. What I had failed to consider was the following week's schedule, which called for a Tuesday game against our toughest opponent. Normally, I would have used our number one pitcher to start and left him in as long as the game was close since we had an easy game later in the week. Unfortunately, however, I couldn't pitch him at all, and we lost the game. If I had just stayed with my original plan the previous week of pitching him three innings in each of both games, I could have pitched him six innings the following Tuesday; but when he pitched four innings in the Saturday game, I had to rest him for three days before he could pitch again.

Deciding how many innings in which to use a pitcher has to be an exercise that you plan carefully, depending on the schedule. If you have two good pitchers, the safest plan is to pitch each only three innings in a game and be sure of having each available for the next game with only one day's rest. The only problem with that plan is that you may take out a pitcher who is doing a great job and replace him with one who can't find home plate. As mentioned earlier, most Little League pitchers don't warm up enough, which becomes an obvious problem when you want to insert a new pitcher in the fourth inning who is already in the game in another position. When does he warm up, particularly if he is on base during the inning before he is to pitch? The only sure solution to the potential problem is to take the time and make the effort to train at least three pitchers. Then, if I have one tough game in a week, I would prefer to have my number one pitcher go as many innings as he can against that team, knowing I have a choice of two backup pitchers for the other game.

One other tip regarding pitchers' warming up: During the game, if your team has been at bat for a long time, or if the game is delayed for any reason, resulting in your pitcher's arm having been inactive for a long period of time, I would try to get some extra time for him to warm up again before he pitches to the first batter in the next inning. Too often your catcher will cut the warm-ups short by throwing to second. You should tell your pitcher and catcher that the *pitcher* should decide when he is ready. Although Rule 8:03 limits preparatory pitches to eight, most umpires will be lenient about this, if they keep count at all. When I umpire, I ask the pitcher if he is ready because I am more concerned with his well-being than sticking to the letter of the rule. By contrast, a new pitcher that you have to bring in cold is allowed "as many pitches as the umpire deems necessary," per the same rule. If the umpire wants to resume play before the pitcher has warmed up enough, most kids will be too willing to accommodate him. I may walk over to the umpire while the new pitcher is warming up and ask him to give the boy plenty of time so he doesn't hurt his arm. Most umpires will be accommodating.

## The Intentional Walk

Another pitching tactic deserves mention because it may win a ball game for you—if it is drilled. It is the intentional walk. If you face a team with an exceptional hitter, but comparatively weak batters that follow him, and he comes to bat with a runner in scoring position and first base open, I would walk him intentionally in most cases. However, to be sure your catcher can catch the four intentional wide pitches, have your catchers and pitchers do some practice drills on this tactic. I called the tactic in a close game with a runner on third and two outs, only to have my catcher leave the catcher's box too soon. (*See* Rule 4.03 [a].) It was called a balk that scored a run. Many Little League umpires would not have called it, but this one did, and he was correct.

## COACHING YOUR RUNNERS

Most coaches don't call time out to coach their runners often enough. Time-outs have both a practical and a psychological effect, giving you the opportunity to tell a runner what you want him to do and breaking the concentration of the pitcher, who will start to worry about what you are up to. There are four situations in which it makes sense to call time out, particularly when the game is close:

### Time Out Prior to a Walk

If you see an opportunity for a fast boy to get into scoring position by making second base on a walk (because no one is covering second, because the catcher and pitcher are not alert, etc.), call time when the count is 3 and 0 or 3 and 1, and remind your batter to check the sign. The opposition will probably think you are just advising him to take the next pitch.

### Time Out on a Steal

If you want a boy to steal and aren't certain that he got the steal sign, call time and tell him, rather than take a chance in a close game. You should have told the batter to fake a bunt on the next pitch to distract the pitcher and catcher and help your runner to second; but if your runner missed the steal sign, your strategy is revealed, and you may have given up a strike against the batter as well. You may argue that you tip off your strategy in talking to your runner, but the psychological effect may offset that. The pitcher and catcher will be worrying about whether it is a bunt or a steal, and when the batter goes into the fake bunt position, they will guess wrong.

I made the point earlier that I will do almost anything to avoid an easy force out at second, which is the reason that I stress using the time out as important base running strategy in getting that lead runner to second base.

## Time Out with Runner on Third

As mentioned in Chapter 6, the opportunity to steal home is much greater in Little League games than most teams realize or take advantage of. You, as coach, must watch the opposing pitcher, third baseman, and catcher every time you have a man on third. The tip-offs are: (1) the third baseman doesn't hold your runner close and/or (2) the pitcher doesn't cover home and/or (3) the catcher, on a short passed ball, throws from the point of retrieval instead of running back to the plate to throw. If you see the potential opportunity and aren't confident your runner is thinking of the steal, then call time and go over and tell him. You may argue again that you will be tipping off the play, but probably not, since you are just reminding your runner what to do *if* the situation occurs. Your opposition may be thinking of a squeeze play, and in any event, it doesn't hurt to keep them worrying about what you are up to, to break their concentration.

Third baseman is not covering after the pitch, which gives the runner a good chance to steal home.

## Time Out with Runners on First and Third with Fewer Than Two Outs

You will want the runner on first to go to second on the first pitch to the next batter and hope the opposition makes a play on him so your runner on third can score. In order for the play to succeed, you should call time out to be sure the three boys involved know what they have to do:

1. *The batter* should fake bunt the first pitch; if he swings at it and lines out, it will be an easy double play with the runner on first on his way to second.
2. *The runner on third* must be ready to go home if a play is made at second, but he must avoid being caught in a cutoff play. His best tactic is to go off base two steps, which he should do in every case, and hold long enough to make sure there is actually a play made at second.
3. *The runner on first* must go on the first pitch but should break late to try to draw the throw from the catcher. If you really need that run on third, you could even tell the runner on first to stumble and fall down between first and second in order to make it difficult for the catcher to resist trying to throw him out.

Naturally, you can't take the time—nor will the umpire allow it—to confer with all three boys on this play. Your best tactic is to have a code name or number for the play, such as "13," and drill it enough in practice that, when you signal it from the dugout, the base coaches and runners on first and third will recognize it and know what to do. I would still recommend calling the batter from the on-deck circle, before he goes to the plate, and reminding him to fake bunt on the first pitch. It is better to sacrifice a possible called strike than to take a chance of his hitting into a double play. It is part of the strategy of getting the runner to second base without risking a force play.

Although you have coached your base coaches to keep reminding the base runners of the number of outs, that other players are on base, to "run on a grounder" when forced, to "run on anything with two outs," etc., a vocal reminder from you from the dugout is still recommended. It not only reminds the runners, but also reminds the base coaches what they should be doing.

## COACHING YOUR BATTERS
### The Fake Bunt

We just dealt with one situation in which the fake bunt would be used: when you want a runner on first to steal second. You don't want the batter to hit the ball for fear of his lining into an easy double play, but you do want him to distract the pitcher and catcher in the hope that it will induce a wild pitch or passed ball and help your runner to get to second without a play.

Another situation calling for a fake bunt is when you want the batter to take a pitch (not swing on it), usually on a 3 and 0 or 3 and 1 count. You want that next pitch to be a ball, so you should have your batter fake a bunt to rattle the pitcher. Most Little League pitchers will tend to throw outside when a batter crowds the plate. It must be an instinctive desire to avoid hitting the batter that makes Little League pitchers do this, as opposed to Major League pitchers, who will brush back a batter who is crowding the plate. In any event, I have seen it happen so many times that I know it is true, and therefore a tactic such as a fake bunt will frequently cause a pitcher to throw an outside pitch and give your batter a walk.

Your batters need to be drilled in the proper way to fake bunt, however, since the tactic could backfire if the umpire feels that the batter is going for the outside pitch and calls it a strike. Because it

Batters must be good actors, too. Here batter is showing fake bunt position by leaning over plate, bringing his bat up and down, trying to coax a ball, a wild pitch, or a passed ball.

is essentially a psychological tactic, your batter should get in a bunt position sooner than he would in a real bunt situation, when surprise is important. He wants the pitcher to start worrying about a bunt early, so he should go into an exaggerated bunting act as the pitcher starts his windup. I call it an "act" advisedly, since that is actually what it is. He faces the pitcher, crowds and leans over the plate, moves his bat up and down menacingly, while the catcher tries, with obvious difficulty, to keep his eyes on the ball. *However, the batter must pull back before the ball reaches the plate,* or the umpire may rule that he was going for the pitch. The tactic obviously requires drilling.

## The Real Bunt

As a neophyte manager, I followed the classic rule of having a batter sacrifice bunt to advance a runner when there were less than two outs. However, in Little League, I soon observed that there were more runners advanced by pitchers who were throwing wild pitches and catchers who were guilty of passed balls than there were by bunters. However, in both instances of sacrifice bunting or bunting to hit, when an inexperienced bunter tried to bunt on the first pitch, he frequently had trouble making fair contact with the ball. If he tried a second time and failed, he was then collared with an 0 and 2 count and was getting more uptight with each successive failure. To add insult to injury, the first and/or second pitch would have been called balls if the batter had pulled back, and he could have had a 2 and 0 count instead of 0 and 2. Meanwhile, the element of surprise is gone as soon as the batter tries and fails to bunt the first time.

Unless your batter is a very dependable bunter, I would advise waiting until the count is 2 and 0 before calling a bunt. That is a good tactic because (1) the element of surprise will be complete and (2) the pitcher has to try to get the ball over the plate, so he may be aiming the pitch, or taking something off it, which will make it an ideal pitch to bunt.

You might even try a squeeze bunt with a man on third on a 3 and 0 count if you have a weak hitter coming up next and you need the run. The pitcher will certainly be aiming his pitch over the plate and should give your batter a fat (ideal) pitch to bunt. If the pitcher throws a bad pitch and your batter pulls back, then he still

Chuck Tanner shows correct bunting hand position to author's son Jim.

gets a walk. In this situation, there are three things that could happen to score a run: (1) the hitter could bunt safely; (2) the pitcher could be distracted enough by the bunt attempt to throw a wild pitch; or (3) the catcher could be distracted enough to allow a passed ball. In any of the three cases, you not only score a run but get a man on first, too. So it's worth a try in the right situation. The squeeze play in that particular situation (3 and 0 count and a weak batter coming up) is about as complex a play as I would ask a Little Leaguer to execute. "Hitting behind the runner," "hit and run," "suicide squeeze," and other such complex plays are too complicated and require practice time that would be better spent drilling the basics in Little League.

## COACHING YOUR DEFENSE

Two observations I have made concerning how Little League play differs from more advanced baseball have a bearing on the way you should position your defense:

*1. More balls are hit to the right side of the field.* This is undoubtedly due to the fact that most Little League right-handed batters are inclined to swing late, especially against fast pitching. What it means in positioning your defense is that you should shift to the right in both your infield and your outfield, and your first baseman should play deep and guard the line. It also means that your second most reliable outfielder should play right field.

*2. Most Little League outfielders play too deep.* I concluded this after watching too many "Texas Leaguers" and bloop singles fall in front of outfielders. The average Little Leaguer, when he hits the ball to the outfield at all, will not hit it far; the exceptions will become well known, and then you can signal your outfielders to move back.

The combination of these facts has prompted me on occasion to employ a shift in which I will do without a left fielder and have the extra fielder play behind second base. That gives you three infielders on the right side and allows your extra infielder to handle backup plays to second base and pop flies to short center. The center fielder, in such a shift, would shade to left, and the third baseman would play deep to compensate for the lack of a left fielder.

## Infield-In Shift

Another defensive maneuver you should drill is the "infield-in" shift. It should be employed when the bases are loaded, to get the force at home, and when there is a runner on third in a close game and you want to keep a run from scoring on an infield grounder.

This defensive play occurs often enough that it deserves to be drilled in practice and called in a game. Your defense may not react soon enough to the situation that calls for it, so you will have to call "infield in!" from the dugout.

## Shortstop Play

Mentioned earlier, this is the cutoff play with runners on first and third in which the catcher throws to the shortstop, who fires the ball back to the catcher to trap the man trying to score from third.

Infield is in to prevent runner on third from scoring.

## Intentional Walk

This tactic was discussed earlier in this chapter (see the section "Coaching Your Pitchers").

## COACHING THE UMPIRES

The title of this section is obviously facetious, but since Little League umpires are generally less knowledgeable of the rules and less experienced than umpires at higher levels of baseball, it is necessary on occasion to do a little subtle coaching in the two situations in which umpires' decisions are questioned.

### On Rule Interpretations

A good coach should always carry a rule book and know it well enough to be able to refer to a rule if a questionable call is made. If you are sure the umpire is wrong, the best thing to do is calmly call time out and quietly show the umpire the applicable rule rather than force a confrontation that will embarrass him. If he won't back down, then you have no choice but to register a formal protest with him. In most cases, however, if the situation is handled calmly, the umpire will reverse himself. If you believe the umpire was wrong in interpreting a rule but can't find the rule in the heat of the situation (it happens!), and the umpire insists on continuing the game rather than taking the time to find the applicable rule, then you again have no choice but to register a formal protest. However, you must register the protest "immediately and before any succeeding play begins," in accordance with Rule 4.19 (c); otherwise, regardless of the merit of your case, the protest cannot be accepted.

## On Judgment Calls

The same rule, 4.19, also points out that "No protest shall be considered on a decision involving an umpire's judgment." The instant replay on TV has occasionally shown umpires' judgment decisions to be wrong, even in the Major Leagues. Usually a bad call is made when the umpire is in a bad position to see the play yet has to render a decision. Because of the lack of training and experience of many Little League umpires, and because many games are played with only two umpires, it is not unusual for an umpire to be in a poor position to make a close call. In such a situation, when you are certain the umpire was wrong, you can ask him to check his call with his fellow umpire, or you can use something better than an instant replay: the opposing team's players. "Little Leaguers don't lie!" is a refreshing discovery I have made about most 9- to 12-year-old Little Leaguers. Two examples make the point. In one of our games in which there were only two umpires, with a man on first, the base umpire stayed at first base, in a poor position to make an outfield call. Our field is enclosed by a low cyclone fence, which creates some problems of depth perception on balls hit to the outfield. Our batter hit a long ball to left center field that went over the fence, hit the ground, and bounced high. From his position behind first base, the base umpire couldn't tell whether the ball hit in front of the fence and bounced over or went over the fence before it bounced. He decided to call it conservatively and ruled it a ground rule double. Our batter was certain it had gone over the fence, but frankly, I wasn't any more sure than the umpire, so I called time and quietly suggested to the umpire that he go out and ask the left and center fielders where the ball hit. He agreed, and when he came back he ruled it a home run. How could the opposing manager object when his players told the truth?

On another occasion, when there was a close call at home plate, our runner was called out, which created a roar of disapproval from our bench and from the spectators, who hurled some juicy barbs at the umpire. As our player returned to the bench, I asked him, "Were you out?" and he nodded "yes," which immediately calmed the storm and elicited a grateful look from the umpire. What is a parent supposed to say to his 10-year-old son who tells the truth? "Why didn't you lie?" I hope none would be so callous.

There are occasions when you know you won't get a reversal on a judgment call but when it still makes sense to question the umpire, if only for the purpose of keeping him on his toes by letting him know you are watching his calls carefully. In another one of our games, the base umpire didn't show up, so the home plate umpire had to recruit someone from the stands—in this case the father of the other team's first baseman. That situation doesn't normally bother me, because I have found that dads who are called upon to umpire usually will bend over backward to be impartial. In this case, however, it seemed like all the close plays at first base were going against our runners in a very tight game. Finally, there was a play in which it seemed obvious that there was at worst a tie between our runner and the ball arriving at first base; yet he was called out. I called time, walked over to the umpire, and quietly said that, since he was a substitute umpire, I thought maybe he didn't know the rule on a tie. He said he knew that the runner was safe in a tie, but insisted in this case that the runner arrived after the ball. I replied that I hadn't seen it that way and returned to the dugout.

Our conversation was very quiet and without confrontation, and although our spectators were beside themselves, they quieted down when I went back to the dugout, apparently satisfied that official attention had been focused on the umpire's calls. It may have been my imagination, but it seemed like all the close calls after that went our way. I call it the "law of umpire averages." But if you don't let *him know* that *you know* he blew one, the umpire won't be motivated to improve his umpiring. You don't have to do it à la Billy Martin, which just makes an umpire resent you; I would rather have him respect me and concede that maybe I had a point.

In another game with another umpire, our batter was hit on the arm by a pitched ball, which also hit the bat. The question was whether it hit the arm or the bat first. The boy was so obviously in pain that it seemed to me that it had hit him first, but the plate umpire called it a foul ball. At the end of the inning, I took the boy over to the umpire and showed him the outline of the baseball on the boy's swollen wrist, which certainly wouldn't have happened in a ricochet. The umpire shrugged, but his eyes said, "I blew it!" We both knew that there was nothing he could do about it at that point, but I hoped that he would remember that he owed us on the next close play.

## KNOW YOUR UMPIRES

In addition to coaching the umpires, you should know your umpires. We called one in our league "Low-Ball Lenny" because of his reputation for consistently calling strikes at the knees. I prefer an umpire who calls them like that from a defensive standpoint, because I want my pitchers to keep their pitches low, especially on the good hitters. However, I constantly have to remind my boys when they go up to bat that "Low-Ball Lenny" is calling behind the plate and to be ready to swing at balls that come in at knee level. Usually an umpire in a low crouch will call them low, and, conversely, a "lazy umpire" who stays up most of the time will miss the low strikes.

In a tournament game, I noticed an umpire who was not from our league was "throwing the flag" frequently on our base runners. After watching carefully, I didn't think a runner had left base too soon, yet he had the flag thrown on him. I questioned the umpire, and he showed me Rule 7.13, which says, "When a pitcher is in contact with the pitcher's plate and in possession of the ball . . . base runners shall not leave their bases . . . ." Because I taught our base runners to be aggressive, they were jumping off base after every pitch, daring the catcher or pitcher to make a play, but on some occasions they were still off base when the pitcher returned to the mound with the ball and touched the rubber. This umpire interpreted that to be a violation of Rule 7.13—that, if the runner didn't return to the base before the pitcher was ready to pitch, he should be considered off base on the next pitch. I didn't agree with the umpire's interpretation, but I explained to my boys what to do, and I reminded them of it in future games in which that particular umpire handled the bases. It was part of knowing your umpires.

## CHARTING TO WIN

A winning coach in every sport has to be a good analyst, and Little League baseball is no exception. I recommend that three

Chuck Tanner with some of the author's players at Three Rivers Stadium in Pittsburgh.

kinds of records be kept to give you the important information to analyze.

## Dugout Scorebook

As mentioned in Chapter 9, I advocate keeping a dugout scorebook, in addition to the official scorekeeper's scorebook, for two reasons:

1. It gives you a quick reference to the progress of the game (what each batter did his previous times at bat, which players are coming to bat in the next inning, etc.).
2. It gives you the opportunity to chart the substitutions your opponent makes and to audit his compliance with the mandatory playing rule.

When the opposing manager gives you his lineup, make sure it is complete, showing fielding positions and uniform numbers of each player, batting order, and names and uniform numbers of all substitutes. As the game progresses, and the opposing manager advises the umpire and/or you of each substitution, make sure you chart in the dugout scorebook the name and number of the boy he replaces in the field (it will usually, but not always, be the same boy he replaces in the batting order). This is important, because the boy who leaves the game may not reenter until his substitute has played six consecutive outs in the field and batted at least once. In a tight defensive game, when the batters go up and down in order, a substitute may be required to play three innings in the field before he gets to bat once, and this may foil the opposing manager's strategy of getting his starting player back in the lineup.

Analyzing your opponent's strengths and weaknesses is a way you can contribute to your team's success. As a standard procedure, I signal to my pitcher the batting order number of the next batter, since he will obviously pitch differently to a weak hitter than to a strong one. In Little League, there is only one way to pitch to a weak hitter, in my opinion. Challenge him with fastballs in the strike zone but, above all, don't walk him. You need your dugout scorebook, with the substitutes charted, to do this. You also need it to analyze the defensive changes when they occur; e.g., if a substitute catcher and/or second baseman is put in the lineup, you can more safely call a steal; same for a substitute third baseman. A new pitcher will be so concerned about pitching well that he may be subject to mental lapses in his fielding, so if the other team brings a new pitcher in with a man on third, for example, you may be in a good position to have your runner steal home on a passed ball, since the new pitcher may forget to cover home. A substitute first or third baseman would be a good target for a bunt.

## Chart of Your Team's Substitutes

Figure 6 is an example of a chart that I prepare *before* every game, showing who plays what position and the batting order for every inning; even the base coaches are included in the chart. Some managers put in all of their substitutes at the same time, theorizing that it's best to get them all in and out and get it over with and not expect to do anything while they are in. In planning substitutions, I recommend they be staggered, for several reasons.

In the first place, it gives me the assurance of having a balanced team in the field at any time. For example, if I put in a substitute at second base, I like to have an experienced boy on either side of him (at short and first). Or in the outfield, I feel comfortable putting rookies in left and/or right field so long as I have a dependable boy in center to back them up and an experienced player in front of them in the infield.

The other reason relates to the development of the rookie's abilities. Both psychologically and actually, he will perform better with experienced players around him. It helps his confidence and, in my opinion, raises his level of competence. We all know the experience in sports of playing up to the level of competition. You always play better in the company of better players.

From a game strategy standpoint, I believe in starting my strongest team and finishing with my strongest team. That means inserting the substitutes in the middle innings and replacing them with the starters in the late innings. To implement that game plan, keeping in mind both game strategy and the mandatory playing rule, requires pregame planning. Rather than depending on a mental game plan, I prefer taking a few minutes, usually the night before the game, to chart my game plan.

An added dimension of managerial skill is introduced when you must maneuver 15 boys in and out of a 6-inning game, abiding by the mandatory playing rule, while at the same time exercising the proper strategy moves to help your team. In a 6-inning game, there are 54 innings of fielding play (nine positions times 6 innings) to be divided among 15 players, an average of 3.6 innings of playing time in the field per player. In Figure 6, I show how I would normally plan the rotation of the players in a game that I expect to be close. My four objectives are:

1. Start with the strongest team and finish with the strongest team.
2. Stagger the insertion of substitutes to keep a well-balanced team.
3. Keep experienced players around a rookie.
4. Make sure that each player plays the mandatory six consecutive outs in the field and bats at least once.

Figure 6 is the chart of a game expected to be close; consequently, it requires the strategy of playing your best players for the

## FIGURE 6.
## CHARTING YOUR TEAMS SUBSTITUTIONS

GIANTS vs YANKEES    5/23
(HOME)   (VISITORS)   (DATE)

BATTING

| Inning / Batting Order | 1 | 2 | 3 | 4 | 5 | 6 | 7 |
|---|---|---|---|---|---|---|---|
| 1 | Mark | Mark | Mark | Mark | Mark | Mark | |
| 2 | Jim | Jim | Jim | Jim | Jim | Jim | |
| 3 | Chris | Chris | Chris | Chris | Chris | Chris | |
| 4 | Paul | Paul | Paul | Paul | Paul | Paul | |
| 5 | Dave | Dave | Dave | Dave | Dave | Dave | |
| 6 | Rod | Rod | Tony | Tony | Rod | Rod | |
| 7 | Chuck | Tim | Tim | Ed | Ed | Dave | |
| 8 | Mike | Mike | Joe | Joe | Jeff | Jeff | |
| 9 | Jeff | Lane | Lane | John | John | Mike | |
| Coach 1st | Tim | Tony | Ed | Tim | Tony | Ed | |
| Coach 3rd | Lane | Joe | John | Lane | Joe | John | |

*FIELDING*

| Inning Position | 1 | 2 | 3 | 4 | 5 | 6 | 7 |
|---|---|---|---|---|---|---|---|
| Pitcher | Mark | Mark | Mark | Paul | Paul | Paul | |
| Catcher | Chris | Chris | Tony | Tony | Chris | Chris | |
| 1B | Paul | Paul | Paul | Mark | Mark | Mark | |
| 2B | Chuck | Tim | Tim | Ed | Ed | Chuck | |
| SS | Jim | Jim | Jim | Jim | Jim | Jim | |
| 3B | Dave | Dave | Dave | Chuck | Chuck | Dave | |
| LF | Jeff | Lane | Lane | John | John | Mike | |
| CF | Rod | Rod | Chris | Chris | Rod | Rod | |
| RF | Mike | Mike | Joe | Joe | Jeff | Jeff | |

maximum amount of time and your rookies for the minimum. For the sake of illustration, I assumed we have 4 key players, 5 other starters, and 6 rookies. You would normally bat your key players in the top four spots in the batting order, so they get the maximum number of times at bat and bat your other players in descending order by ability. The relative playing time of your 15 players, based on these assumptions, will be as follows, as charted in Figure 6.

| Player's Position in Batting Order | Number of Innings in Which He Will Field and Could Bat |
|---|---|
| 1 | 6 |
| 2 | 6 |
| 3 | 6 |
| 4 | 6 |
| 5 | 4 |
| 6 | 4 |
| 7 | 4 |
| 8 | 3 |
| 9 | 3 |
| *Substitutes:* | |
| 10 | 2 |
| 11 | 2 |
| 12 | 2 |
| 13 | 2 |
| 14 | 2 |
| 15 | 2 |

In Figure 6, my first goal has been met—that of starting with my strongest team in the first inning and finishing with the same team in the sixth.

My second goal was staggering the substitutes, and that has been met with two entering in the second inning, two in the third, and two in the fourth. (In order that you can easily follow the insertion of the six substitutes, I have numbered and circled them, 1 through 6). The third and fourth innings will be the weakest innings from a team standpoint since four substitutes will be playing at the same time in both innings, balanced by five regulars. Since those are normally the innings in which your opposition will also be playing its substitutes, you are not really risking any disadvantage.

My third goal has also been met in having the rookies backed up by regulars.

My fourth goal of meeting the mandatory playing requirements for all players has two potential weak spots that I must keep in mind, namely, the eighth and ninth batters in the starting lineup, Mike and Jeff. Mike will get his six consecutive outs in innings one and two and will bat if we send eight boys to the plate in the first two innings. If not, then his only chance to bat is in the sixth. If I see that is not probable, then I will have him pinch hit for one of the boys who has met his mandatory playing requirements in the fifth or sixth inning. In Jeff's case, my ninth batter, there is an even greater risk of his not meeting the mandatory requirements since he is removed after the first inning and not reinserted until the fifth. If he didn't get to bat in the first and there appeared to be a possibility of his not meeting both requirements in the fifth and sixth, then I would have to substitute him in the fourth for a boy who has met his mandatory playing requirements. Since both Mike and Jeff are starters, the worst consequence of making a change in the plan would require reinserting a starter an inning earlier than planned, which isn't much of a sacrifice.

I stated that Figure 6 is the plan for a game expected to be close. If the game becomes lopsided by the fourth inning, you could leave the substitutes in the game and bring your starters back in to replace one or more of the first four boys in the lineup, in order to balance the playing time among all of your boys. My game plan against any easy team will obviously allow the rookies more playing time.

When our local league expanded to 10 teams, we cut back the roster limit from 15 to 14, which allows more flexibility in charting the substitutes. Whatever the roster size, there will always be games in which one boy or another will not be able to play because of sickness, vacation, or other legitimate reasons. That will also give you more flexibility in planning your substitutions. I ask my players to be sure to let me know by the night before a game if they aren't going to play, so I don't waste time on a chart that includes them. Even so, I always have several blank chart forms with me at a game in case of a last-minute no show that requires me to revise the chart just before the game.

## Chart of Your Team's Statistics

I ask one of my coaches to be our official scorekeeper at each game and to make up our team statistics at the end of every three games. An example of a team statistical chart is shown in Figure 7. One of the ways you would use this chart would be in establishing your lineup. Before your first game, you will have to make your lineup based on preseason assumptions about your players, but as the season develops, you should be ready to make changes in your lineup based on facts such as performance statistics rather than on assumptions.

The first four batters in the lineup should be the boys who have the best records for hits and walks, because they are in the batting order positions that will get the most times at bat. If the statistics contradict your preseason assumptions, you should change your batting order accordingly. For example, I have changed my leadoff man when the statistics have shown me that another player is leading the team in walks and rarely strikes out—two excellent qualifications for a leadoff man. In another instance, the statistics of a player showed that he was getting too few walks; he was so anxious to get a hit that he was going after bad pitches instead of making the pitcher give him pitches in the strike zone. The statistics will quickly point out the boys who are striking out the most and need more batting practice.

In addition to helping you coach your team better, the statistics will serve as an additional motivator for your players. They will naturally want to improve their percentages. However, there is a danger that the statistics will have a negative effect on a boy who isn't doing well, if the purpose behind the statistics is not explained. You should emphasize that the stats are a record to show each individual's improvement during the season and that you won't tolerate any criticism by a teammate of boys whose stats don't look good. The important thing is that each boy show improvement in his statistics, and you are pretty safe in establishing that as a ground rule, because rarely does a boy not improve his stats as the season progresses.

## WINNING WITH SPIRIT

There can certainly be no denying that emotion can motivate a team. The emotion of winning can be very strong and very contagious to a team that is on a roll—and very demoralizing to the opposing team.

Team spirit is an intangible thing; you know when your team has it, but knowing how to develop it is another matter. The familiar "We're number one" chant, used by every team that has ever won one or more games, is so phony that it falls flat with Little Leaguers, who are pretty perceptive about spotting and rejecting phony things and people.

There is a lot of emotion in a Little League game—most of it the negative emotions of fear and uptight nervousness that are natural for youngsters experiencing their first taste of competitive pressure. I believe an important reason for trying to instill team spirit in a Little League team is to counteract and overcome those negative emotions. I think it is helpful to pump up your players, getting their spirits high to counteract the butterflies before a game starts, but it is more important to sustain it during the game. I recommend using the routines below during a game to stimulate team spirit.

## Team Chatter

In my opinion, there is no better way for defensive players to counteract the butterflies than to keep up a steady stream of chatter the whole time they are in the field. I also believe that there is nothing as reassuring to your pitcher as a steady stream of chatter backing him up. Finally, I believe that there is nothing more effective in breaking the concentration of a batter than a steady stream of chatter that crescendos every time he has a strike called on him. The chatter has to be positive, not directed negatively toward the other team or its players, and it isn't as important what the players say in their chattering as it is that they keep it up. Particularly when things are going well for your team, the chattering seems to help sustain the momentum. When things are not going well, it helps them regain their confidence. I have found that it helps to find, or train, a vocal team leader on the field who cheerleads the chattering. My choice would be the catcher because he is facing the rest of the team and can be seen and heard

## FIGURE 7. GIANT AVERAGES, FIRST HALF (9 GAMES)

### BATTING

| PLAYER | G | TAB | W | HP | S | OAB | H | TOB | R | 2B | 3B | HR | RBI | SO | BATT. AVG. |
|---|---|---|---|---|---|---|---|---|---|---|---|---|---|---|---|
| Lane Acree | 7 | 14 | 0 | 0 | 0 | 14 | 6 | 6 | 4 | 0 | 2 | 0 | 2 | 5 | .429 |
| Jim Beirne | 9 | 33 | 5 | 0 | 0 | 28 | 10 | 15 | 11 | 0 | 3 | 0 | 8 | 5 | .357 |
| Rod Blankenship | 8 | 19 | 2 | 0 | 0 | 17 | 6 | 8 | 6 | 1 | 0 | 0 | 5 | 4 | .353 |
| Rodney Cox | 9 | 13 | 3 | 1 | 0 | 9 | 2 | 6 | 0 | 0 | 0 | 0 | 0 | 6 | .222 |
| Jeff Girod | 9 | 13 | 1 | 1 | 0 | 11 | 5 | 7 | 2 | 2 | 0 | 0 | 0 | 2 | .455 |
| Mike Grose | 7 | 9 | 1 | 0 | 0 | 8 | 3 | 4 | 3 | 1 | 0 | 0 | 2 | 1 | .375 |
| John Hoard | 9 | 20 | 4 | 0 | 0 | 16 | 6 | 10 | 3 | 1 | 0 | 0 | 0 | 3 | .375 |
| David Joo | 9 | 25 | 4 | 0 | 0 | 21 | 11 | 15 | 8 | 0 | 2 | 0 | 7 | 4 | .524 |
| Mike Lipscomb | 9 | 17 | 2 | 1 | 0 | 14 | 5 | 8 | 3 | 0 | 1 | 0 | 3 | 8 | .357 |
| Jim McIntosh | 9 | 34 | 6 | 0 | 1 | 27 | 15 | 21 | 12 | 1 | 0 | 0 | 6 | 4 | .556 |
| Mark Proctor | 9 | 35 | 5 | 0 | 1 | 29 | 17 | 22 | 13 | 2 | 0 | 1 | 9 | 0 | .586 |
| Chuck Thomas | 9 | 16 | 1 | 0 | 0 | 15 | 7 | 8 | 3 | 0 | 0 | 0 | 6 | 2 | .467 |
| Mike Walton | 9 | 17 | 3 | 1 | 0 | 13 | 2 | 5 | 3 | 0 | 0 | 0 | 0 | 10 | .154 |
| Paul Williams | 9 | 30 | 5 | 0 | 0 | 25 | 12 | 17 | 9 | 5 | 2 | 1 | 13 | 6 | .480 |

KEY: G (Games); TAB (Total times at bat); W (Walk); HP (Hit by pitched ball); S (Sacrifice); OAB (official times at bat); H (Hits); TOB (Total times on base); R (Runs scored); 2B (Doubles); 3B (Triples); HR (Home runs); RBI (Runs batted in); SO (Strike outs); Batt. Avg. (Batting Average -- number of hits divided by official times at bat).

**PITCHING**

| PITCHER | G | IP | BF | R | H | W | HB | SO | R/P |
|---------|---|----|----|---|---|---|----|----|----|
| Jim Beirne | 7 | 19 | 85 | 14 | 10 | 12 | 8 | 26 | .78 |
| Mark Proctor | 4 | 9 | 32 | 5 | 5 | 6 | 0 | 12 | .56 |
| Paul Williams | 8 | 22 | 101 | 17 | 7 | 26 | 5 | 49 | .77 |
| Mike Lipscomb | 1 | 3 | 14 | 2 | 0 | 5 | 0 | 7 | .66 |
| Chuck Thomas | 1 | 3 | 12 | 0 | 1 | 3 | 0 | 4 | .00 |

KEY: G (Game); IP (Innings pitched); BF (Batters faced); R (Runs scored against); H (Hits given); W (Walks given); HB (Hit batters); SO (Strike out); RIP (Runs per inning).

by them. He can also intimidate a timid batter with his barrage of encouraging chatter to the pitcher.

## Strikeout Routine (with No One on Base and Fewer Than Two Outs)

A strikeout for your pitcher is an emotional high in the game that you should capitalize on. I recommend the routine of having the catcher fire the ball to the third baseman as the rest of the infield folds around the pitcher. The ball is relayed around the infield, back to the third baseman, who hands it to the pitcher. By that time, the entire infield is around the pitcher, encouraging him, patting him on the back, etc., before the players run back to their fielding positions. It is a show of confidence and support to your pitcher, and it is a technique that has been known to strike fear in the heart of the next batter.

## Infield Out at First (with No One on Base and Fewer Than Two Outs)

This is a similar routine, with the first baseman relaying the ball around the infield—first to short to second to third and back to the pitcher. Both this technique and the strikeout routine have the added purpose of keeping your infield loose, which is particularly important in a game with little action.

## Outfield Out (with No One on Base and Fewer Than Two Outs)

This is also a similar routine, with the outfielder throwing the ball to the relay man after the catch, who then whips it around the infield. All three routines are familiar to anyone who has watched a Major League ball game. However, you seldom see it used in Little League. The first time I tried these routines, the boys were very awkward when they tried them and forgot to do them most of the time, so we gave up on them. I finally realized that they are like any other routines; they need to be drilled in practice in order to work. I believe these routines are valuable enough in sustaining team spirit during a game to justify the practice time required.

## Team Huddles

Although I ridiculed the "We're number one" chant, I do like to use something to counteract the butterflies before a game starts. I will sometimes use a team huddle and say, "Play hard, play fair, have fun," and the players will break the huddle with "Let's go!" After two consecutive championship seasons, I was faced with a rebuilding job with eight rookies the next year. I kept reminding them they were playing on the championship team and asked them as we got ready to take the field, "Who were champs in '80?" They came back with "The Giants!" Then I asked, "Who were champs in '81?" and they came back again with "The Giants!" Finally I asked, "Who will be champs in '82?" and got a resounding answer, "The Giants!" It helped to get them to believe they could do it, even though the odds were against it, but they were in contention until the final week of the season with a team spirit that was far greater than their abilities; it was the classic case of "the higher you reach, the higher you will achieve!"

## Using Psychology

Sometimes you may have to use a little psychology to stimulate one emotion to counteract another. In one tournament game, I got verbally rough on the team because I sensed they were uptight and it was affecting their game. So I decided to create the emotion of anger and told them how bad they looked; that they should be ashamed of themselves, letting a no-stuff pitcher strike them out; that they should "kick themselves in the butt" and get mad enough to win. In the end, I wasn't sure whether they were angry at me or at themselves, but they were mad when they stormed out of the dugout, no longer uptight, and they won.

You need to use good judgment in how best to break the tension, since being too rough on the players could do more harm than good. Sometimes a joke will relax them more. We had one boy who always got uptight when he was getting ready to bat. I found that a good-natured reminder that his girlfriend was out there watching him always brought a big smile, some friendly kidding from his teammates, and a relaxed atmosphere rather than a tense one.

In addition to working on team spirit, you will have occasion to work on individual spirit to bring out the best in the lazy boy, the

Nothing will give your team an inspirational lift like having one of your boys hit a home run. Have your team ready to give him a "high five" to keep the momentum going.

hothead, the hotshot, the loner—each of whom can have a negative effect on building team spirit. You would have to be a good amateur psychologist to reach them all, but it is worth the effort and makes the extra time and trouble worthwhile when you do reach a boy. We had a pitcher who wore his emotions very close to the surface, and I sensed in a particularly close game that he was so uptight that he might blow up if anything went wrong. I took him aside between innings and asked him to help me keep the team from blowing it if anything went wrong, like an error or a lucky hit. I reminded him that, as pitcher, he was the team leader and had to keep his cool so the rest of the team would keep theirs. He said he understood and would do his best to help me, and he did. He set an example for keeping his cool that the rest of the team sensed and followed.

## Humor: A Valuable Tool

You have to maintain a sense of humor as a Little League coach, because there will be many situations in dealing with unpredictable children when you will need it. Sometimes it can help to ease the tensions of a game. For example, we were playing in a county tournament in which tournament rules were in effect; i.e., the mandatory playing rule was waived, and boys taken out of the lineup could not reenter the game. I had been warned to keep at least one substitute player on the bench to avoid a forfeit situation, but we were winning, and I wanted all of the boys on the team to share in the victory, so I inserted my last substitute in the lineup. A little later, my heart sank when one of my regulars, who had allergy problems, called time and came running across the diamond to me. In a game earlier in the season, he had done this when he developed a severe migraine headache from his allergy medicine and had to leave the game. All of our players tensed up, recognizing the potential problem, then broke up when he blurted out, "I have to go to the bathroom!" Fortunately, the umpire was accommodating, but the humor of the situation relaxed the team's tension in that game and in many subsequent games, when all I had to do was say, "Rodney, have you gone to the bathroom lately?"

## COACHES AS ROLE MODELS

My final advice to a manager or coach who wants to lead his team to becoming a winner is to set a personal example. Never forget that you are dealing with children—impressionable children who are easily influenced by role models. If you think your team lost because of "lousy umpiring" and say so, your boys will believe it and repeat it. If you say you lost to a good team, they will accept it, even better than you will.

I never said that winning was always measured in terms of championships; as a matter of fact, I mentioned that my most satisfying year as a manager was when we came in third with a rookie-loaded team that drilled hard enough, believed enough in themselves, and had enough fun in the season that none of them or their parents would have concluded that we were anything but winners!

Providing good perspective was my goal in sharing my Little League coaching experience with other dads who have the privilege of working with their son's team. When your son and his teammates remember their Little League years as times of learning athletic skills, as times of learning teamwork, and above all, as times of having fun—then you can be proud of having been a winning coach!

# INDEX